THOUSAND NAMES OF VISHNU

★

He is all, and the beginning of all things.
He is existence, its cause and its support.
He is the rays of the moon and the light of the sun.
His forms are many, but he is hidden.
His face is everywhere.

Thousand Names of *VISHNU*

A Selection with Commentary by
EKNATH EASWARAN

NILGIRI PRESS

ISBN paper: 0–915132–46–X
cloth: 0–915132–47–8

First printing October 1987

The Blue Mountain Center of Meditation, founded
in Berkeley in 1960 by Eknath Easwaran, publishes
books on how to lead the spiritual life in the home
and the community. Please write for information to
Nilgiri Press, Box 477, Petaluma, California 94953.

Library of Congress Cataloging in Publication Data
Easwaran, Eknath
  Thousand Names of Vishnu / Eknath Easwaran
    p.   cm.
  ISBN 0–915132–47–8   0–915132–46–X (pbk.)
  1. Viṣṇusahasranāma – Commentaries.   2. Vishnu (Hindu
  deity) – Prayer-books and devotions – History and criticism.
  I. Title.
BL 1138.V57E5   1987   294.5'211—dc 19   87–28225
                                                          CIP

Table of Contents

5

Table of Contents

Table of Contents

Table of Contents

Table of Contents

Introduction:
The Thousand Names
of the Lord

Most of the world's major religions have a tradition celebrating the Holy Names of God. Muslims have the *Most Excellent Names*; Christians have litanies and commentaries like that of Saint Bernard. Jewish tradition preserves several lists of the Divine Names, which Jewish mystics have made the focus of meditation. The Holy, the Merciful, the Compassionate; Truth; the One: these are names which appear in each religion, emphasizing that however we call him—or, as in some parts of my native India, *her*—the Lord is always the same.

In Hinduism, one of the most popular of these litanies is *Sri Vishnu Sahasra-nama Stotrum,* the "Thousand Names of Vishnu." Since no concept can ever describe the Infinite, Hindus believe that the Lord has many forms—Shiva, Ganesha, the Divine Mother, and so on—shaped, so to say, by the inner needs of those who worship him. The *Thousand Names* praises God as Vishnu, the preserver and sustainer of life, worshipped all over India in his incarnations as Krishna and Rama.

I must have heard the *Thousand Names* recited a thousand times while I was growing up. My grandmother, my spiritual teacher, would place a lighted oil lamp in front of the image of Sri Krishna. Then an uncle who was a Sanskrit scholar would chant the names of the Lord one by one, with the sacred word *Om* before each name and the word *namah* after it. "*Om Vishnave namah!*" It means "I bow to Lord Vishnu," "I worship Lord Vishnu," much like the Christian or Jewish "Blessed art thou, O Lord." With each name my uncle would take a fresh lotus petal, touch it to his heart, and offer it at the feet of the Lord. This is *japam,* repetition of the mantram or Holy Name, as it has been practiced throughout India for centuries.

I was not a very devotional boy, and I have to confess that rituals meant little to me. But after an hour of this kind of recitation at dawn with my family, the *Thousand Names* used to echo in my mind for the rest of the day. Even without reflection, the meaning went in. The Lord is *everything,* everywhere; he dwells in every heart:

> *Om!* I worship Lord Vishnu,
> Who has become the universe and pervades all.
> Lord of past, present, and future,
> He has made and supports all that is.
> He is being and the essence of all beings;
> He is the pure and supreme Self in all.
>
> He *is* all, and the beginning of all things.
> He is existence, its cause and its support.
> He is the origin and the power.
> He is the Lord.
>
> He is the One from which creation flows.
> His heads are a multitude, yet he is the Self in all.
> His eyes and feet cannot be numbered.
> Many and mighty are his forms.
>
> His soul is revealed in light; as fire he burns.
> He is the rays of the moon and the light of the sun.
> His forms are many, but he is hidden.
> He has hundreds of forms, hundreds of faces;
> His face is everywhere . . .

Even for a child, then, the *Thousand Names* were a constant reminder that there is a spark of divinity in everyone. It prompted us to be a little more considerate, a little more kind, a little more selfless with those around us—which, I suppose, is just the effect these rituals are supposed to achieve. Filling your mind with the thought of God is not primarily an esthetic experience. It has a very practical purpose; for what we think of constantly, we see wherever we look.

Later, as an adult, I discovered that ritual is not necessary to achieve this goal. The most effective form of *japam,* in fact, is the silent repetition of the Holy Name or mantram in the mind: *Jesus, Jesus,* or *Rama, Rama,* or *Allah, Allah,* or whatever formula has been sanctified by tradition. This form of prayer has been taught in every major religion, and in my experience it is second only to meditation as a tool for transforming consciousness.

In the following pages, I have chosen a fraction of the Thousand Names and added a practical commentary on what each name means in daily living. These comments are based on the eightfold program for spiritual growth which I have followed in my own life and have taught in this country for more than twenty-five years. Meditation is the heart of this program, as it is of my life; so I refer to it constantly in the pages that follow. What I mean by "meditation," and how I differentiate it from the repetition of a mantram, are explained in the brief summary of my program at the end of this book.

THE THOUSAND NAMES

The "Thousand Names of Vishnu" comes from the *Mahabharata,* an ancient epic poem which is a vast treasury of Hindu legend and literature—including the best known and most universal of the Hindu scriptures, the Bhagavad Gita. In this epic setting, the *Thousand Names* is given to the philosopher–prince Yudhishthira by a great sage named Bhishma. The prince asks his teacher a question that must find an echo in every heart: "How can I find joy that will always be with me, satisfying my deepest desires?" Bhishma's reply is to reveal the Thousand Names, with the assurance that if they can be repeated in the deepest reaches of consciousness, this continuous "prayer of the heart" will fill the mind with joy.

Each of these names carries significance. Some refer to the power and beauty of the Lord; others recall some incident in the vast mythology of Vishnu, whose compassion sustains the world. As Vishnu, "he who is everywhere," God has entered into all creatures as their innermost consciousness. He upholds the cosmos from within, as its ruling principle, and establishes and embodies *dharma,* the indivisible unity of life.

In Indian mysticism, which has a genius for clothing the Infinite in human form, Vishnu embodies the source of beauty and order in creation. His body is the dark blue of limitless space, and the galaxies hang from his neck like innumerable strands of jewels. His four arms show that he holds sway over the four quarters of the world. His are the qualities that draw forth love: forgiveness, beauty, and a tender compassion for all creatures.

Vishnu's image is found in temples, shrines, and homes all over India. Usually he is represented as a handsome man of divine radiance who holds in four hands the symbols of power and beauty. A necklace of precious gems adorns his neck. When he travels he is carried by the cosmic eagle, Garuda, or rides a chariot drawn by four spirited horses. In rest he reclines upon the serpent called Infinity, floating in the cosmic waters in perfect peace, dreaming the dream of the world. Though benevolent, he is noted for a mischievous sense of fun. He is universally kind, always approachable, understanding, and serene. The imagery surrounding Vishnu is of light and peace.

Vishnu is also God the protector, who rescues humanity in time of need and supports and strengthens us from within when other resources fail. He is infinite, but from time to time throughout history his love for his creation is so great that he allows himself to be born as a human being to show the world a way out of evil and suffering. Rama and Krishna are the best loved of these divine incarnations. Krishna, in fact, is so completely identified with Vishnu that the two can be regarded as one and the same—as I do occasionally in the pages that follow.

The name *Krishna* is said to come from the root *krish,* meaning to attract. Krishna is God with a human face, and his enchanting smile attracts all things. He is usually portrayed as a youth, in the years when he was a cowherd boy in the idyllic village of Vrindavan. A peacock feather shimmers with beauty in his long hair, which flows around his face like the blue-black rain clouds that blot out the tropical sky during the monsoon. With his body gracefully bent and his arms holding a flute to his lips, he plays an irresistible song. He wears yellow silk, and a garland of wildflowers swings from his neck; on his chest dances a sacred jewel.

This is how Krishna is painted by his devotees as an incarnation of Vishnu. The imagery is specific, but the beauty and compelling attraction of this Lord of Love is universal. Krishna is the spark of divinity in every heart, constantly calling us to return to him. As long as we are alienated from the Lord within, we will be restless and unfulfilled; for this divine spark is our deepest nature, the innermost core of our being. The Lord of Love, present in every human heart, is our real Self.

Swami Ramdas, a very appealing saint of South India whom my wife and I had the privilege of meeting many years ago, used to say that the name of the Lord *is* God. This is a dramatic way of emphasizing that when you realize the full significance of the Holy Name, you have realized the unity of life. All your desires will have merged in the love of God, whose presence you see in everyone around you. In this sense the Holy Name is a key that can gradually unlock the prison of separateness which confines and isolates every human heart. It can lead us to the discovery of our true personality, eternal, immutable, infinite, and pure.

In Indian mysticism the Lord is said to be *satyam, shivam, sundaram:* the source of all truth, all goodness, and all beauty. When we open ourselves to this source of glory within, a part of it pours into our life. But in order to do this, we have to get ourselves out of the way. We have to learn to defy and eventually to extinguish all the passions by which we make ourselves separate from others: anger, greed, lust, self-will.

This is a tremendous challenge, but repetition of the Holy Name is an infinitely powerful ally. As the mind fills with the thought of God, the heart becomes pure; for as Bhishma says in the *Mahabharata,* the very name of the Lord is a purifying, transforming influence. Anger gradually turns into compassion, greed into generosity, lust into love.

All this Bhishma explains to Prince Yudhishthira, so that he can hear each Holy Name with full understanding of its significance. Then, having prepared Yudhishthira to receive them, Bhishma says, "Now, O prince, I shall recite the Thousand Names. Listen carefully, and they will remove fear and evil from your life."

Thousand Names of Vishnu

He Who Is
Everything

VISHVA

We are apt to think of the universe as something apart from God, as a product that has nothing to do with divinity. But the *Thousand Names* reminds us from the outset that the Lord *is* the universe. He has entered into all things. At the core of creation, in the heart of every creature, is the Lord, the very basis of existence.

In this sense the world is not so much the creation of the Lord as an emanation *from* him. The Upanishads, India's most ancient scriptures, say that just as a spider spins a web out of itself, so the Lord has spun this entire universe out of his own being.

Imagine a spider sitting in the middle of her web. She doesn't go away once she has made it; that is her home. This is the analogy the Hindu mystics use, only they take it one step further. At the end of time, they say, the Lord will draw the web of the universe completely back into himself. Christian mystics use similar language: we come from him, we rest in him, and to him we shall return.

Because we have come from the Lord, all we have to do to see him is to look within ourselves and discover who we really are. This is the ancient cry of Socrates— *Gnothi seauton,* "Know thyself"—and in spite of the progress of modern civilization, it is a cry we still need to hear. The human condition is to look just the other way: outside, away from ourselves, to find meaning and fulfillment in the world of the senses. This is the subject of a beautiful passage in Browning's poem *Paracelsus*:

Truth is within ourselves; it takes no rise
From outward things, whate'er you may believe.
There is an inmost center in us all,
Where truth abides in fullness; and around,
Wall upon wall, the gross flesh hems it in,
This perfect, clear perception—which is Truth.

A baffling and perverting carnal mesh
Binds it, and makes all error: and to *know*
Rather consists in opening out a way
Whence the imprisoned splendor may escape,
Than in effecting entry for a light
Supposed to be without.

Today it is almost impossible to believe that the source of joy could lie within us. But no human being can really be satisfied for long by going through life mechanically, picking up a little pleasure here and a little prestige there, while everywhere insensitive to the needs of those around.

We are so conditioned to believe that happiness can be gained by accumulating money and manipulating others that we can't see how ridiculous a belief this is. If gourmet living were the source of joy, then it would follow that the more we eat, the happier we would be. If money were the source of security, then the more we had, the more secure we would be. To be honest, I don't know of anyone for whom this is quite true. Yet we go on believing that somehow, someday, *we* will break the pattern and find what we are looking for outside us.

He Who Is
Everywhere

In the Vedas, the ancient source of the Hindu tradition, appears the great saying, "There is no one in the world except the Lord." If we take it seriously, this is a sobering thought. At no time can we get into our car and drive to a place where we can afford to be selfish. Everywhere we go the Lord is present. If extraterrestrials arrive from the far reaches of the Andromeda galaxy, we may not know anything about their language or civilization, but we can be sure that the Lord lives in them. If we go to Moscow and listen to a speech in Red Square, however fervently the speaker might insist that life obeys no law but dialectical materialism, we can be sure that the Lord is within him, listening to his words with an amused smile. The Lord is the Self, say the mystics, and the divine ground of all existence. Life is one and indivisible in him, and a place where he is not is inconceivable.

It takes a lifetime to grasp the significance of this simple truth that the Lord is present everywhere. But as it seeps into our consciousness, we gain a new respect for all creation. When we *know* that the Lord lives in everyone, for example, violence is out of the question; it is a violation of the unity of life. Like Mahatma Gandhi, we may feel impelled to take up battle against violence and war, beginning by setting a personal example.

Similarly, when we see that it is the same Lord who lives in Africa and Asia and South America, we see that the welfare of other nations is part of our own. If we see people going hungry in other parts of the world, we will be incapable of hoarding for ourselves. Sharing the resources of the earth generously with everybody becomes an aspect of spiritual living. No one has put it more eloquently than Jesus: "I was hungry and ye gave me meat; I was thirsty and ye gave me drink. . ." When we are feeding the hungry we are feeding the Lord, and when we use more than is necessary, we are depriving the Lord. Realizing that the Lord is present everywhere thus impels a gradual simplification of our life. It not only benefits others; it brings us too a new degree of health, security, and freedom.

Many centuries ago in India, in the state of Madras, lived an eminent woman mystic named Andal. On one occasion Andal had spent the night in the home of some devotees, and when the woman of the house came to wake her up, she found her guest lying with her feet toward the north. She was shocked and confused, for in some sections of Hindu society the Lord is considered to dwell in the Himalayas and pointing or touching with the feet is a sign of disrespect. But Andal only replied: "In what direction shall I point my feet? If I point them to the north, true, the Lord is there. But if I point them to the south, is he not there? He is also in the east and west. Shall I sleep standing on my head?"

Similarly, there is nowhere we can go to leave the Lord behind. At no time can we afford to lock ourselves in a closet and say, "He is not here, so I can be selfish. I can do whatever I like."

Often we are so concerned with the activities of the day, the little things that irritate us or the little pleasures we desire, that we lose our sense of proportion. We forget there is anything beyond the breakfast on our plate. Here the mystics try to remind us that "he who is everywhere" is not only enshrined in our heart, but pervades the entire cosmos.

Here we see the real magnificence of this name *Vishnu*. On the one hand, we human beings occupy a speck of a planet around a very ordinary sun out in the suburbs of the Milky Way galaxy, whose billions of stars make a great wheel about a hundred thousand light years across. Astronomers now believe there are billions of such galaxies in the observable universe, and no one can say what lies beyond the threshold of our observation. Yet no matter how far we extend our frontiers, the Lord will still be there, reaching beyond the farthest we can reach and still remaining in the hearts of all.

Maker of All Beings

All of us, whatever our past, are sons and daughters of the Lord. That is why Jesus taught his disciples to begin their prayer with the words *"Our* Father." When we eliminate every trace of separateness from the Lord, we find ourselves united with one who is not only our Father but also, as we say in India, our Mother too.

This is not merely union but a reunion. Like the prodigal son, we have returned to the Lord after many years of wandering, to find the peace and security which can only elude us when we look for them outside. "There is no joy in the finite," the Upanishads say; "there is joy only in the infinite." Our capacity for joy is infinite, and anything less than infinitude can only leave us hungry and unfulfilled.

Meister Eckhart, the great German mystic, explains this vividly. All of us, he says, have the seed of God within us. Just as a farmer has to plant the seed, water it and nourish it, weed around it and protect it, so we have to develop our spiritual potential by systematic hard work. If we watch an apple tree over many seasons and see it producing thousands of apples, we can say that the potential for these apples was in the single seed from which that tree sprang. In the same way, we should remember that the God-seed is in all of us, waiting for the water and warmth and proper soil to quicken it into growth.

This makes everybody special. We all have a little label

inside us, "Made in heaven." Through years of self-centered conditioning we may have almost rubbed it out; but if we look carefully we can make out a few letters: "———h———v–e-n." If we haven't quite made the best of our lives, it can be very reassuring to remember that nothing we or anyone else can do can take away this label of innate goodness. But at the same time, the point is that this label is in everyone. If we say "*I* am special," or "My family or race or country is special," the innuendo is that everyone else is second class. In fact everyone is special, because we are all the handiwork of the Lord.

This vision can be extended to animals too, and in that lies the basis of vegetarianism. When you have become aware of the unity of life, you see that the calf and lamb are as precious as your dog or cat. You see them as companions to be loved and cherished, and their safety and freedom become yours.

William Blake wrote:

> The wild deer wandering here and there
> Keep the human soul from care.

Deer often wander across our property in the country, even grazing right outside my window in broad daylight. Gradually they are losing their fear and discovering that this is a place where they are safe. The sight fills me with delight. When I see these gentle creatures finding refuge here, I think of a monastic friend in India who used to tell us that sometimes, when he was meditating alone on the slopes of the Himalayas, he would be so still and peaceful that deer would come and rub their antlers against his shoulders. This is how far the unity of life can go. When we see the unity that joins us to what we are pleased to call the "lower creation," all creatures sense that awareness. This is the truth Saint Francis was teaching when he preached to the birds or converted the wolf of Gubbio.

The Support of All Creatures

BHUTA-BHRIT

The Lord within is our true support, our only real source of security. This has tremendous implications for personal relationships. As long as we do not know our real Self, our inner foundation, we are always likely to be grasping at others for security. When we do not have a sense of security within ourselves, we easily become agitated when others say or act contrary to our desires.

One of the surest signs of spiritual growth, then, is losing the desire to possess people. Relationships improve immediately, because this desire to possess is what damages personal relationships. Nobody likes to be possessed. Imagine putting a little stamp on your boyfriend's collar: "Name: Romeo. Owner: Juliet, Verona." When I see that stamp, I know it is only a matter of time before that relationship falls apart, unless Romeo and Juliet learn new ways of thinking. No one really wants to possess and be possessed. Our real need is to be one, to be united. This is the meaning of love and romance, which possessiveness misunderstands and misapplies.

When we realize this, we relate to others in a completely new way. Instead of looking for our own fulfillment alone, we begin to look for the good of those around us as well. When people act negative, we have the support within to be more patient, more loyal, more understanding. This is how we gradually erode the walls of the ego-prison of selfish desires that separates us from others. When the walls are gone, we are at home with everyone; nothing can shake our security.

The Supreme Self

The Lord is the essence of every person in the universe, what Emerson called the Oversoul. Here we must understand two aspects. Even though God is one and indivisible, he lives in every one of us; so he appears to be many. Yet at the same time, this supreme Self is not contained by any individual or any created thing. The cosmos itself cannot contain him. In the Bhagavad Gita, by far the best known of India's scriptures, the Lord says, "I am in everyone, but no one is in me." God dwells in everyone, so we must respect his presence in all life; but at the same time we should remember that he transcends his creation completely. In the terms of theology, these are the immanent and transcendent aspects of the Lord.

The Self in Every Creature

This word *atma* or *atman* means simply "self," and I know of no better name for the Lord in any language. He is our innermost personality, the divine spark that is dearer than our very life.

This name reminds us that the Self within us is the same in all creatures. In the climax of meditation, when all the selfishness that divides us from the Lord is dissolved and we discover this Self in the depths of our consciousness, at that moment we see the Lord in every other creature as well. These are not two different discoveries, in other words; they are different aspects of the same realization. To find out who I am, then, is to find out who you are—and who everyone else is too.

The One

This is one of the simplest names for God in any tradition. The Upanishads say that God is *eka eva advaitam*: "one without a second." The Lord is the only one in the universe; he doesn't have any competition. Who or what could compete with him? He is alone, though masquerading as the many.

Herbert Benson, a medical doctor who has studied the health benefits of using the mantram, has published a book recommending the repetition of the word "one" in meditation because this is a word without any religious connotation. In fact, not only Hindus, but Christian, Jewish, and Muslim mystics, have used this simple word as a name of God, and Plotinus preferred it almost exclusively. So although most of us would find it rather dry, it is not without spiritual significance.

The name *Eka* reminds us that there is nobody who doesn't have a spark of the divine within. When we act or speak unkindly, it recoils on ourselves: we are being unkind to the Lord, who dwells in the hearts of all. Jesus says, "As you have treated even the least of these, so you have treated me."

The Many

With the name *Eka,* the Lord tells us to call him "One." Then he comes through another door and we don't recognize him. We ask again, "What's *your* name?" And he says, *"Naika"—na eka,* literally "not one," which is a Sanskrit way of saying "many." So the Lord is up to his usual tricks. He is one and everyone all at once.

This apparent paradox is the result of looking at the same reality from different points of view. From one perspective the Lord is the one reality underlying all of life. But when we view this supreme reality through the senses, the mind, and the intellect, which can only deal with separate objects, we see only the superficial appearance, and unity appears to be many.

This is called *maya,* the illusion of separateness, or *lila,* the divine game that the Lord of Love plays, in which the One appears as the ever-changing, ever-varied multitude of creatures. He plays as five billion human beings, but that is not all. He plays as the beasts of the field, the birds of the air, and all the other creatures that inhabit this universe.

The Hindu tradition has many stories to remind us of the value of every creature, no matter how humble. Many of these stories tell of figures like Ganesha, whose elephant form personifies the Lord's power to remove obstacles from our path, or Hanuman, the powerful monkey who was devoted to Rama, an incarnation of Vishnu. But there are also many stories about lesser creatures which don't get such a good press. In the *Ramayana,* the great epic poem in which Hanuman is almost as much the hero as Rama himself, there is a heroic eagle who gives up his life in an attempt to rescue Rama's wife, Sita, from the demon king. And when Rama goes to get Sita back, he is accompanied by an army of monkeys and bears.

There is even a wonderful vignette in this story about a squirrel, who sees Rama grieving over the loss of Sita and is so moved that he wants to help. At that point Rama's forest army is engaged in building a bridge of huge boulders across the ocean, and everyone would have understood if Rama had replied gently, "What can a little squirrel do?" But Rama knows that everyone has a contribution to make. One by one, the squirrel brings his stash of nuts and tosses them in among the boulders. Rama was so touched by the "squirrel's mite" that he stroked the back of the tiny creature with his divine fingers—and that, they say, is why the Indian squirrel to this day has three stripes down its back.

Maker of All Things

VISHVA-KARMA

The Lord is the cosmic architect, the universal builder—
the designer, the contractor, the blueprints, and the
building development too.

I like to interpret this name playfully as the cosmic
carpenter, who has built this house, the cosmos, not only
for us earthlings but for billions of galaxies to share.
Unlike ordinary building projects, this one is ongoing;
there is always something to do. Every morning Sri
Krishna goes out the front door with his carpenter's tools
and a hefty box lunch. "Don't expect me till late," he
says. "Some of those galaxies still need a lot of work."
Why not? Jesus was a carpenter too. The point is that we
don't need to pay homage to the bricks and mortar and
two-by-fours for housing us so expertly; we would do
better to thank the builder. "Everybody praises the building," says Sri Ramakrishna, a towering mystic of
nineteenth-century Bengal. "But how many seek to
know its Maker?"

The Essence of All Beings

It is worth a few moments of reflection to grasp what it means to say that God has become all things. In an age that tinkers with genes and speculates about the first three minutes of creation, we may forget to wonder about the world we live in and how little of it even our sciences can grasp.

We know, for example, that light travels at about 186,000 miles per second. We know that fact, yet it is quite another thing to understand it. Imagine, as young Einstein did, that you had a long ray of light like a commuter train, and that you could sit astride this ray as you sit on the five-fifteen express and travel at the speed of light. It would take only a second and a quarter to reach the moon; one blink of an eye and you would be there. In eight minutes—the time it takes to get to the nearest supermarket—you would reach the sun. Yet you would have to sit there on that magical ray for four years to reach the nearest star, and you could travel that way for one hundred thousand years and never get out of our same old Milky Way. Imagine the expanse! Then for two million more years it is just empty space—no gas stations, no Holiday Inns—until you reach the nearest neighboring galaxy. There are believed to be two hundred billion galaxies within the observable universe, each of them containing perhaps a hundred billion suns. It's not even the whole picture, yet we still can't grasp it; we can't absorb what these figures mean.

33

Suppose, one science writer suggests, that you are willing to work eight hours a day, seven days a week—no days off to tend to the yard—counting at the rate of one number every second. It will take a month to reach one million, a relatively small figure on our scale. If you want to understand one billion, this writer says, keep counting in the same way—no coffee breaks, no vacations, no union slowdowns—until the end of your life. I said to myself, "Yes, sir, I get the point."

Most intriguing, perhaps, is why astronomers are so careful to say "the *observable* universe." It doesn't mean only "That's all we can see for now," as if some day, with more powerful telescopes in orbit beyond the moon, we might be able to see it all. If Einstein was right, as a good deal of careful observation still bears out, then we can never "see" the whole universe. The speed of light itself limits us to a kind of bubble of observation in space-time, beyond which we simply cannot perceive. No messages can reach us from beyond that bubble, and none can be sent. But that does not mean there is nothing beyond; these are merely restrictions on the delivery service.

Worse yet, as soon as we start looking any significant distance into this bubble, we find we are seeing things not as they are but as they were. Wherever we look in the starry sky, we are looking quite literally at the past. One star appears to lie next to another, but actually we see each of them as it was when that light set out on its journey. One of those stars might have been destroyed centuries ago in the explosion of a supernova; we cannot know. We devote special attention to a star, analyze its spectrum to see what it is made of, guess at its past and future evolution, and while we are guessing, that "future" has happened and the star may be gone! If it is a thousand light years away, the news of its death would not reach us for a thousand years. The Crab nebula represents the remains of a supernova explosion observed by Chinese astronomers in A.D. 1054, but the actual explosion took place about 3000 B.C. Even the constellations whose names have come to us down the ages may suffer from severe generation gaps: the stars in them may be separated by thousands of years, as we measure from here on earth. Space and time, bound together, inevitably limit and distort the validity of what we can say about the universe.

But these dimensions do not apply to the Lord. In the Hindu scriptures we find the provoking statement that this vast cosmos is one thought of the Lord. That is as long as our universe lasts: one thought.

The Eternal Law

DHARMA

It is an axiom of mysticism and science alike that this vast, complex universe, so impossible for the mind to grasp as a whole, follows one set of laws. The universe is a unity, so the same laws hold everywhere: and that unity, the source of all law, is another aspect of the Lord.

Wernher von Braun has said that outer space is not a hostile place but very friendly, so long as we know and observe the laws that apply there. Similarly, this essential, law-abiding unity of life makes the cosmos a friendly place, so long as we understand its rules. Until recently, it seems, many scientists accepted the view that we are isolated here on earth in a barren, hostile universe. They pictured our planet traveling forlornly through empty, alien space. These attitudes have changed. What takes place a few thousand miles over our heads is anything but meaningless for human life. You don't have to travel to the moon to pick up a moon rock: just pick up any old rock; it is made of the same atoms as a rock from the Crab nebula, the same atoms as your own body. The depths of space are ruled by the same forces which govern life on earth. "A planet capable of sustaining life," as one German scientist commented, "did not come into being independently of the rest of the universe."

The cosmos is not only vast; it is also dizzyingly complex. Our earth, to take just one example, rotates on its axis in four minutes less than twenty-four hours; and while it spins, it is revolving in its own six-hundred-

36

million-mile orbit around the sun. On top of that, the earth wobbles as it performs these feats; its axis slowly gyrates through one turn in about twenty-six hundred years. Then we are told that the sun itself is hurtling along toward some inexplicable rendezvous in the Milky Way, while the whole Milky Way galaxy whirls majestically about a center of its own—and, in addition, does its best to move away from all other galaxies with ever-increasing speed. It reminds me of circus gymnastics, like those feats where a woman in spangles gallops around the ring straddling two horses while she juggles torches in a circle of fire.

Yet in all this complexity there is complete harmony. Everything follows dharma, the basic principle that all of existence is one whole. The cosmos is like a huge dance floor where everyone is Ginger Rogers or Fred Astaire; nobody gets out of step. Every body in the cosmos—galaxies, quasars, quarks, black holes, suns, moons, stellar dust—quietly moves in harmony with the cosmic order, which is the same here on earth, on Mars, around Alpha Centauri, everywhere.

This is serious business, for even the slightest disequilibrium could destroy us. How many times do we hear ourselves saying, "Put out the trash? I just forgot. I'll do it tomorrow." Suppose the earth felt that way about its responsibilities. "You can't expect me to remember *every*thing. I was trying to get the precession of my nodes just right and, well, I just forgot about going around the sun!" The Lord says simply, "This won't do." Everything has to obey his laws; that is a condition of existence.

Lord of Past,
Present & Future

BHUTA-BHAVYA-BHAVAT-PRABHU

This is a reminder of the law of karma, which no one has stated more succinctly than Jesus: "With whatever measure ye mete out unto others, with the same measure it shall be meted out unto you." The Lord is ruler of the past, present, and future because it is his law, the law of life, that whatever we did in the past has to shape our present, just as whatever we do today must shape our future. Just as there are laws governing the motions of heavenly bodies, there are laws that apply in our own lives, laws which we can break only at our peril. To maintain good health, for instance, we have to learn to use our bodies properly. Sooner or later, those who disregard the fundamental laws recorded in the very cells of the human body must suffer the consequences of bad health. How many of us damage our health by smoking or overeating, by hurry and competition in our work, by nursing hostility or anger? In one view, diseases of the lungs and other vital organs are random tragedies. The mystics would say no; they are the natural result of violating natural laws.

Though this may sound harsh, the mystics make a very encouraging comment: if our thinking and acting today shapes our tomorrows, then the future lies to a significant extent in our own hands. The Lord does not sit above us, judging us and decreeing rewards and punishments for our actions. Our actions themselves carry within them the seeds of pleasant or unpleasant results.

This is the principle behind the law of karma. According to this law, whatever situation we find ourselves in today, we have contributed to that situation by all the desires and fears, the acts and aspirations, of our past. If we have lived a wrong life, it is only natural that our health should be poor, that we should have emotional problems, that we should find it difficult to relate to people.

This is not the Lord punishing us. We have created the situation for ourselves. But if we got ourselves into a mess, we can get ourselves out. The surest evidence of the Lord's compassion is how swiftly a deep, heartfelt change in our ways of thinking and acting today can bring a better tomorrow.

This point of view is very liberating. For the present, it admits, we have to bear the burden of the past. We have all committed mistakes and tried wrong methods of living, so there is a certain amount of unpleasant consequences that we have to face today. But by changing our habits, by reminding ourselves that we and others are one, by training ourselves to think more of the needs of the whole and less of our own private desires, we can change our future into one of health, security, joy, love, and wisdom.

In the utmost depths of meditation, when all the distinctions of space and time dissolve, we pass from time into the eternal Now. Therefore the Lord is said to be the ruler of time, past, present, and future. After all, past and future are not real except insofar as we carry them around in the present, in the form of emotionally charged memories, desires, hopes, and fears. Going beyond time means that all these fall away, and with them go a great many personal problems. "This emptying of the memory," says Saint John of the Cross, " . . . is in reality a great good, because it delivers souls from much sorrow, grief, and sadness, besides imperfections and sins."

The Immeasurable

Not only can we not comprehend the Lord, we cannot even comprehend his handiwork. He is *Aprameya*, "that which cannot be measured," cannot be grasped, cannot even be imagined. Mystics compare God to an ocean that cannot be fathomed, but Shankara, the towering mystic of the eighth century who reawakened India to its spiritual heritage, reminds us that even to compare him with something is to limit what is limitless. Words and thought, trying to approach him, turn back frightened at the frontier of what can be conceived.

The Hindu tradition has a genius for conveying these profound truths through deceptively simple stories. Many episodes in the life of the boy Krishna remind us that although he seems like any other boy, playing with his friends and getting into trouble now and then, there is another dimension which is revealed in the twinkling of an eye when the veil of maya, the illusion of separateness, is pulled back for a moment.

One day little Krishna decides to steal freshly-made butter from his mother's kitchen and distribute it to his friends. When Yashoda walks in and sees Krishna handing out her butter and yogurt to his gang, including the village monkeys, she decides it is time for drastic measures. Krishna is so lovable that he always manages to sweet-talk himself out of disciplinary action. This time he is not going to get away with it. She is going to tie him up until he promises to behave himself.

Yashoda finds a piece of cord and starts to wrap it around her divine imp. But the ends of the cord will not reach. She gets a longer piece of rope, ties it to the first, and tries again. Still it isn't long enough. And all the time Krishna just sits there, trying his best to look contrite but barely able to suppress a grin.

Yashoda brings yet another rope, this time long enough to tie up a cow. Still Krishna remains free because the rope is not long enough. No rope can ever tie him because he is immeasurable. Finally he takes pity on the long-suffering Yashoda and allows himself to be tied up. The infinite Lord can be tied by love; nothing but devotion can secure him.

Yashoda has tied him to the mortar she was using to churn curds. Krishna, needless to say, is not without resources, and he soon manages to get out of this embarrassing position. He sees two trees growing nearby and drags the mortar between them. Such is his strength that both trees come down with a crash, bringing the whole village out to see what the noise is. As it turns out, two spirits had been imprisoned in these trees, and Krishna's escape has released them. Praising his compassion, they fly off to the heavens.

Seeing this miracle, Yashoda and all the villagers marvel at the divine nature of the child they had taken for merely human. Then Krishna deludes them with his maya once again, appearing before them as any ordinary child. But Yashoda has forgotten why she ever was angry with him.

Peace

"Peace" here means not political concord but the profound peace that comes in the deepest stages of meditation, the peace that "passes understanding." When the mind desires no more desires, but rests in the Self, the Upanishads say, that is the state of perfect peace. "As an eagle, weary after soaring in the sky, folds its wings and flies down to rest in its nest, so does the shining Self enter the state of dreamless sleep, where one is freed from all desires." The Upanishads describe our restless lives as the efforts of a bird that flies hither and thither, never finding rest until it settles down in its own nest at last.

These stupendous concepts may sound philosophical, but they have a very practical application. As Pascal exclaimed, "Not the God of philosophers!" Realization of God means "certitude, joy, peace."

After a lot of sustained, systematic effort in meditation, we may finally succeed in breaking through the surface crust of consciousness. What lies below is the unconscious, which has many layers—strata on strata deposited by habits of thinking and acting, little by little, every day of our life. Drilling through these strata in meditation means overcoming limitations, all the obstacles created by self-will: the fierce, driving compulsion to have our own way, get what *we* want, stamp ourselves separate from the rest of life. The biggest leap in meditation comes when we run headlong and throw ourselves over the rim of all duality to land in the unitive state, where nothing is separate from the Lord. This state is *shanti,* perfect peace.

42

Giver of Peace

Most of us have so little peace in our hearts that we direly need this peace of the Lord's. Even in our most intimate personal relationships, our usual attitude is an exercise in civil law; half the time we are the plaintiff and the other half the defendant. We go about saying "He did this to me" or "She said that to me" or "It's not my fault!"—all simply because we lack detachment and get blindly wrapped up in our own pursuits. Caught in ambition or jealousy, we go about playing the role of Macbeth or Othello, suspicious of everyone around us.

The Buddha's approach is easy to understand. When we get angry with someone, he says, we are punishing ourselves; anger is its own punishment. When we are being jealous or self-willed, we are punishing ourselves; jealousy and self-will are their own punishment. When we act self-willed, we don't need any court to come and sit in judgment on us and mete out a sentence: "Two months in the jug or five hundred dollars fine or both." We ourselves are the judge, the jury, and the executioner.

Take, for example, the person who is angry. The proof of the punishment is in the physical changes that take place. Every time that person becomes angry, his breathing rhythm is thrown off, his heart races, his blood pressure rises, and all the chemicals of stress are dumped into his body. If anger becomes a habit, the body becomes conditioned to these physiological reactions, and chronic health problems can develop over time. It is the same with digestion: the person for whom anger has become a habit is subject to all kinds of digestive problems.

Last, most frightening of all, are the effects of anger on the nervous system and the heart. Whenever I see someone getting angry, what I see with my spiritual eye is one thousandth of a heart attack, one thousandth of a seizure. Medical evidence is beginning to bear this out; it is no exaggeration. And this is just to mention the physical consequences; the damage in strained and broken relationships hardly needs illustration.

Again, far from being pessimistic, this view has positive implications. Because we are the entire court ourselves, we can change the proceedings. We don't have to go on playing plaintiff or defendant; we can take the stand as the internal witness. When we begin to find out who we really are, we see everyone's needs more clearly, including our own. We gain compassion for our own mistakes, and compassion for the mistakes of others as well. Then, though we try to correct our own behavior, we will not criticize our little personal version of Othello or Macbeth, because we understand how our responses to past events shaped the direction of the drama. Childhood, neighbors, school, friends, all were factors in what made our life into what it is today. In the same way, we will not criticize others, because we know how powerful the influences are which lead people to make mistakes.

When we have the detachment to recognize some of the sources of trouble in our own lives, we see clearly that love sometimes means saying no when those around us are about to make a mistake that will bring sorrow to them and others. This kind of tender opposition is one of the biggest challenges of the spiritual life. When we see our partner or our friend or our children making mistakes, most of us are afraid to say anything for fear of stirring up trouble. We tell ourselves, "Well, it's a free country." Our concern is not really with freedom; we are simply afraid of the other person's response. A true friend is one who has the faith and loyalty to put up with a harsh response, and who will continue to oppose resolutely and tenderly.

In the long run, this kind of opposition always leads to greater respect. Our friend may not speak to us for a week or so, but after he has a chance to see things more clearly, he will realize that here is a person who cares more for his best interests than about blame or praise.

My grandmother was fond of repeating something that it took me many years to understand: "A good friend should be like a mirror." One side of the face, I am told, is supposed to be more attractive than the other. Imagine a mirror that showed us only the more attractive side of our face, the brighter side and not the darker side. We wouldn't call that a mirror at all. A good friend, similarly, should show us both sides of our personality.

Then she would add, "It hurts me if you get sick, or if you are insecure, or if you don't have your own respect." Here again she would have me in a corner. Like most teenagers, I occasionally had to hear my grandmother tell me things like "Ramaswami from the corner house doesn't have a very good opinion of you." I would answer, "What does it matter what Ramaswami thinks?"

"His sister says you and your cousin are not very polite."

"What does it matter what his sister says?"

Then she would say, "What about your own respect? Does it matter what you think of yourself?"

"Oh, yes, Granny."

"Well, then," she would say, "if you want your own respect, you have to earn it. You can brush off Ramaswami and his sister, but you can't brush off your own self."

Everybody's respect can be easily gained except your own. The Self is the most taciturn, the most difficult, the most impossible observer to curry favor with, because he doesn't need anything and doesn't miss a trick. He has seen everything. You can flatter him any number of times; he will turn a deaf ear. You can offer him tantalizing presents; he will turn a blind eye. And even if you have done enough good deeds to impress the whole

world, even if you have resisted so many selfish temptations that the local weekly prints your picture with a
glowing review, the Self will just wait. "Let us see," he
will say "Let us see if you go on growing, day after day,
year after year, or if you get tired and give up."

That is why there is nothing more exhilarating than
getting a little pat on the back from within. At the end of
a long, hard day, when nothing has gone your way and
you have had to struggle just to keep your composure
from disappearing down the drain, you will sometimes
feel this pat from within and hear the Self whisper, "Well
done."

The Eternal

The supreme reality has always existed and will always exist. It is this very reality which we find to be our real nature when we break through the belief that we are physical creatures, governed by the limitations of the body, mind, and intellect.

"You were never born," says Sri Krishna in the Bhagavad Gita; "therefore you will never die." You, the real you, is not separate from that which existed before your body came into being, before even the sun was born. How can that which was never created cease to be when your body dies? This is the experiential discovery we make in the great climax of meditation called *samadhi* (*sam* "with," *adhi* "Lord"), when we become united with the Lord of Love who is enshrined in the depths of our consciousness.

Happy

After these grand ideas, the *Thousand Names* comes up with a touch of humor.

All of us are familiar with affectionate nicknames. When you want to be intimate, you probably don't address your boyfriend as Benedict. You call him Ben or maybe even "Benny, dear," or you use some pet name that conveys all kinds of private nuances. Similarly, after telling us that his name is Mr. Immeasurable, Mr. Incomprehensible, the Lord must have a wisp of a smile playing on his lips when he says, "But you can just call me Nanda, the Happy Kid."

Nanda means the ground and source of all joy. To attain this supreme state of joy, which brings fulfillment of all personal desires, we have to learn to see the Lord in every person we meet. This vision brings a million times more joy than intimate union with any one individual. Yet at the same time, it brings great responsibility too. When you see someone suffering, it is *you* who are suffering. This identification releases the motivation to do everything you can to relieve that suffering. On the one hand, your sorrow is multiplied a million times; but on the other hand, you have the immense joy of relieving others' pain and sharing their burdens, which is the greatest source of joy on earth.

Toward the end of his life, Saint Francis is said to have retired into the wilderness of Mount La Verna, where he devoted himself fervently to solitude and almost ceaseless prayer. He sought two gifts: first, to feel so far as possible the love Christ felt for all creatures; and second, so far as possible, to feel the suffering Christ endured for all, which is what that love entailed. The two go hand in hand. Brother Leo, Francis's sole companion on that awesome retreat, tells us that after thirty days and nights of prayer, just before sunrise, Francis entered a deep state of ecstasy in which his desires were fulfilled. His identification with his Lord was so complete that like Jesus, the "man of sorrows," he shared the agonies and joys of all mankind.

Few of us dare aspire so high, but everyone is searching for a joy that will never leave. To me, the telling aspect of sensory pleasures is not that they are bad for us but that they do not last. Pleasure is a sensation, and sensations last only for a moment. Nothing in the world can make them stay. We may think we want permanent pleasure, but what we thirst for is not a sensation but a state of being in which all desires are fulfilled. That is joy, a dynamic state in which tremendous resources are released from within to help alleviate the sorrow of the world. We have the unanimous testimony of mystics East and West that this state of limitless joy, love, and wisdom is the birthright of every one of us.

The Unitive State

YOGA

Yoga, which comes from the root *yuj* meaning "to unite," is a word with many meanings. Yoga is both end and means. It is the state of perfect union with the Lord, who is within; it is also the path to this state of spiritual completion.

In this sense there are several different schools of yoga teaching various disciplines for Self-realization. Preeminent is the ancient system of Indian philosophy called Yoga, best represented by the *Yoga Sutras* of Patanjali, which emphasizes the practice of meditation. What is usually called "yoga" in this country is actually a system of physical culture, intended only to prepare the body for meditation.

· If *yoga* means union, the word implies that most of us are suffering from a kind of internal disunity. This division in consciousness is the central paradox of the human condition. We respond to what is beautiful, but on the other hand we feel attracted to things that bring ugliness. We admire somebody who is unselfish, but we have powerful urges to be selfish ourselves. We want abiding joy, but we cannot help going after fleeting, frustrating pleasure.

All these are symptoms of a deeper split in our consciousness which tears us apart. And because we are being torn asunder inside, we express our pain in anger, fear, greed, competition, jealousy, and other negative emotions. It is this inner split that yoga heals—not on the surface but at the deepest levels of the unconscious, where most other methods only tinker with the problem on the surface.

Most people have grown up believing that this primordial urge for union can be fulfilled through sex. This is because we live in such a physically oriented civilization. The more physically oriented we are, the more sensate we will be; and the more sensate we become, the more unshakable will be our belief that sex can heal our loneliness and fill the emptiness in our hearts. Many people honestly believe that it is through sex that two lovers can be united, despite what every sensitive person knows: that whatever we may desire from it, basing a relationship on sex will sooner or later tear those two people apart.

Sex is a sensation. Love is a state of being, a lasting relationship which we can slowly make permanent. That is the deepest desire in all of us, to make this state of union permanent. When we are selfless, in those moments when we feel how close we have come to another person, we taste the joy of love. At these times the split in consciousness is narrower, healing and resolving tensions deep within. Meditation and allied spiritual disciplines—the eight-step program at the end of this book is an example—are together called yoga because they give us a path we can follow to make this union permanent.

It is the desire to prolong these moments of union into a lasting state of consciousness that is caricatured in the attempt to prolong sexual pleasure for two or three minutes more. Much has been written on this subject, and much research has been done in the name of science. There are manuals to show you just what steps to take to enhance your physical relationship—what kind of music to play, what kind of lighting, what scents to put in your bath. It is cleverly done, but it takes all the beauty and all the sanctity out of sexual union. And along with that, it has also taken its fulfillment. This is a caricature of our real desire, which is to attain a loving relationship that will never end.

In this sense, yoga is the divine marriage that takes place between the human soul and our real Self. In everyone this supreme Person is present, whether we call him Krishna or the Christ or call her the Divine Mother. In trying to live in harmony with all, we are moving closer and closer to this marriage with our real Self.

Sri Ramakrishna describes a glorious experience of union with Christ. He had been studying the life of Jesus, whose personality captivated him, and one day in meditation he saw the radiant figure of the Christ coming closer and closer until he walked into Ramakrishna and merged with him. This identification can come to all of us if we dedicate ourselves completely to this supreme goal. When we finally celebrate this divine union, all inner conflicts will be healed, and that terrible chasm in our consciousness will cease to exist. Then we live in our natural state of love, which is the state of perfect yoga.

Spirit

Purusha literally means "person": the supreme Person who is our real Self and, at the same time, Lord of the whole universe.

By folk etymology, *purusha* is said to mean "he who dwells in the city (*pura*) of the body." Hindu scriptures often refer to the body in this way, as a kind of walled city with nine or eleven gates: the senses and other bodily openings. The Self is the *Isha* of this *pura,* the Inner Ruler that dwells within and governs our activities.

One practical implication of this name is that this body of ours is a kind of temple or shrine. We have an obligation to take care of it and keep it clean, and not fill it up with substances that do it harm. But we should always remember that we are not the body but Purusha, pure spirit. No matter how well we care for it, the body, like all things physical, has to pass away someday. We, the Self, can never die.

This Self is the same in every creature that has life. The Upanishads say of the time of creation:

> He made towns with two feet;
> He made towns with four feet.
> Then the Person entered into those towns.

This simple truth is the basis of vegetarianism.

The Supreme Self

Purusha is "person," the Self; *uttama* means "highest." The Lord is the supreme Person, the highest being in the cosmos. There is nothing loftier than union with him; there is nothing beyond union with him. We can reach our highest goal, attain our greatness, find complete fulfillment, by becoming united with this supreme Person who is our real Self.

Here is Meister Eckhart guiding us on how to attain this state of union:

> To get at the core of God at his greatest, one must first get into the core of himself at the least; for no one can know God who has not first known himself. Go to the depths of the soul, the secret place of the Most High, to the roots, to the heights; for all that God can do is focused there.

He Who Has Beautiful Hair

KESHAVA

This is one of the favorite names of Krishna. In India we are very appreciative of long, luxurious black hair. It is considered a sign of great beauty, especially in my native state of Kerala.

The Upanishads say that the universe has grown out of the Lord as hair grows out of the body. The simile is both simple and profound. The universe is not separate from the Lord, but it is not identical with the Lord either. My hair cannot claim that it is me. But at the same time, can I say that it is entirely not me? As your hair is a part of you, the Upanishads say, you are a part of the Lord. All of us grow from him and draw our lives from his pure being.

The Thief

This name is said to derive from the root *hri,* which means "to take" or "to steal." Hari is he who has stolen our hearts. Having created us to roam in the world of separateness and change, the Lord then stole our hearts so that even while wandering we would long to return to him. Because he has kept our heart, we can never find our happiness anywhere else. As Augustine says, "How can I find rest anywhere else when I am made to rest in thee?"

Hare (pronounced *ha-ray*) is the form used when the Lord is called on by this name, as in the ancient Hindu mantram which was my grandmother's:

> *Hare Rama, Hare Rama,*
> *Rama Rama, Hare Hare,*
> *Hare Krishna, Hare Krishna,*
> *Krishna Krishna, Hare Hare.*

This mantram calls on the Lord with three of Vishnu's most familiar names.

Patience

This is one of the most important of the Thousand Names, because it is so practical. My friends often tell me, "You can talk more about patience any time you like. It's something we always need to hear."

Why do we hear so little about patience today? There almost seems a conspiracy in our modern civilization to counsel just the opposite: be impatient, be angry, "look out for number one." But what is life without patience? What use is money if we live in exasperation with those we love, if we cannot stand to live with our own family? What good is it to have your picture on the cover of *Time* if you cannot be patient with yourself? So many songs are written about love; I would like some enterprising songwriter to sing the praises of patience, without which love is impossible.

In Sanskrit we have a beautiful saying, *Kshama virasya bhushanam*: "Patience is the ornament of the strong." What a wonderful idea! Not swords or guns or medals, but patience. We seldom realize what power there is in patience. All the energy consumed in exploding against others, in retaliating, in unkind words, in the anger that brings grief to others and ulcers to ourselves—all that energy can be harnessed as positive, creative power, simply by learning patience.

This is strength that is irresistible. It is the same power that Mahatma Gandhi harnessed in leading India to political independence without firing a shot. If we could exercise this power in our personal relationships, it would transform our lives and make our homes citadels against violence.

One obvious place we can learn patience is with older people and invalids. Grumbling, complaining, and suffering are part of being sick. It is a privilege to serve those who are unwell and to put up cheerfully with an irritable remark. Similarly with older people. It is good to remember that old age will come to all of us, and when your body is not able to function well, the slightest effort can bring pain. At such times it is very difficult to be generous. Spiritual awareness teaches us to serve someone in this condition cheerfully and lovingly: it helps them, and it helps us grow as well.

Another place to learn patience is in taking care of small children. Infants, in particular, have no language except crying. They can't look at their watch and say, "It's half an hour past my mealtime and I'm famished," or take their cereal off the shelf, repeat their mantram, and eat. So they scream. That's their way of attracting attention, and if the response is not prompt, they scream louder and longer. It's not very easy to be patient and cheerful with a screaming baby on your hands; but that is just what makes it the perfect opportunity.

Nighttime, of course, is best of all. In India, where babies sometimes do not have a room of their own, nighttime can really be a problem. The baby will be in one corner of your room, the brother and sister in a second corner, a cousin who has come to the city for a job interview may be on the couch. And in the middle of the night your baby starts crying. Perhaps he has a stomach problem, perhaps he has an earache; maybe he just wants to play. After all, a baby doesn't see the logic of sleeping all night. "Here it is one o'clock and I'm wide awake. Why are all these people sleeping?" He starts expressing the feelings of the moment, and everybody in the house gets upset.

At a time like this, the only way to remain patient is to repeat the mantram or Holy Name and remember the unity which binds everyone in the family into a whole. This is what spiritual living really means. The whole purpose of meditation and other spiritual disciplines is to strengthen us so that we can deal successfully with the trials of life, large and small.

A story about Saint Francis of Assisi illustrates the joy this kind of self-mastery can bring. One day, on a journey across the Italian countryside with one of his dearest disciples, Brother Leo, Francis exclaims: "Brother Leo, even if all the friars were perfect examples of holiness, even if they taught and healed and performed all kinds of miracles, this would still not be perfect joy."

Leo asks eagerly, "What *is* perfect joy?"

Francis, who knew how to make a point and how to tell a tale, replies, "Even if we could understand the birds, and speak with angels, and know all the secrets of nature—even then, Brother Leo, this would still not be perfect joy."

They walk along a little farther, with Francis going on and on like this, until finally Brother Leo gets lovingly exasperated. "Please tell me what perfect joy is!"

And Saint Francis tells him, "If we reach the next town by midnight tonight, cold and hungry and tired, and the gatekeeper tells us that we can't come in, that we are just a couple of ruffians, and he uses all kinds of bad Italian and beats us and drives us out—if we can remain patient and loving through all that, then we shall have perfect joy."

Imagine someone who cannot be disturbed even if you are rude or unkind to him. Imagine someone who moves closer to you when you get angry, instead of running away; someone who keeps showing respect even when you try to strike out and hurt him. Simply being around such people is a joy. Their patience rubs off. Gradually we want to be like them. When we have a selfish impulse, we reject it; we have seen something higher. Once we have an ideal like this to live up to, we try to stretch ourselves a little every day; we see opportunities in every challenge.

Patience

When you reach this stage, all boredom goes out of life. There is no time to feel unoccupied; all your waking moments are devoted to realizing who you are—who is the real Person who lives in this body of yours. You find choices everywhere: Shall I live for myself, doing what pleases me even though it may not be very useful, or shall I give my time to helping others and pursuing the goal of life? As patience grows, you develop the capacity to make these choices in everything you do. Then you will find your spiritual growth swift and sure.

Lover of His Devotees

The Lord loves all creatures, but those who love him with all their hearts have an innate power to draw his love in return. As Saint Teresa of Avila says, *Amor saca amor*: "Love draws love."

This is an especially appropriate name for Krishna, who has a particularly warm corner in his heart for ordinary people who live in the world yet try to remember him. These are the Lord's householder or lay devotees. They haven't left the world, as monastic devotees do; they keep their jobs, live right in the middle of family and society, but do their best to base their lives on spiritual values and disciplines like meditation and the repetition of the Holy Name.

In the Hindu scriptures there is a story about a character named Narada, who is not a householder but a sort of immortal monk. Narada likes to travel about from ashram to ashram stirring people up with spiritual gossip: "In this ashram three people attained illumination last week! In that ashram they are meditating around the clock." Narada appears like this in many of our stories, and the consequences are always instructive.

Once, it is said, Narada asked Sri Krishna, "Lord, why do you like these householders so much? They're not very regular in their practice. One moment they resolve to become very spiritual and the next moment they forget all about it."

Sri Krishna pretended to think a while. "Narada," he

61

said, "I want you to do something for me. Will you take this little oil lamp and carry it around the temple three times? Then I'll answer your question. But don't let the lamp go out."

As soon as Narada took the lamp outside, Krishna called up the winds and said, "Now, blow!" Soon Narada felt hard pressed. The north wind started blowing and the south wind started blowing, and there he was with this little oil lamp he couldn't let go out. But being illumined and immortal, he wasn't completely without resources. He held the lamp close and huddled over it to shield it from the wind, and somehow he managed to get around the temple three times with the flame still flickering. When he finally got back to Krishna, he was a little disheveled but still undaunted. "Well, Lord," he said, "here is the lamp."

Sri Krishna smiled. "Tell me, Narada, while you were going around the temple, how many times did you repeat my name?"

Narada hemmed and hawed. "With all this storm blowing, the north wind and the south wind . . . actually, Lord, I didn't really remember."

"Narada," Lord Krishna said, "these householders have so many problems, what with television, and babies crying, and Madison Avenue to contend with, the wind is blowing against them all the time. If they are able to remember me only a little part of the day, I am very pleased."

Who Makes Love Increase

PRITI-VARDHANA

Everyone wants to be a great lover. Through the practice of meditation, anyone can learn. All that is required—which, I admit, is terribly difficult—is to transform everything negative in our personality into the positive qualities we admire in great men and women of God like Mahatma Gandhi and Teresa of Avila.

This is not done overnight, and it is not done by painting pictures or writing poems about self-transformation. It is done over a period of years by exercising our will and learning to love others more than we love ourselves, beginning with those who are nearest to us.

Today we talk a great deal about love. It is supposed to be the theme of thousands of movies and songs. But in all these things I find very little that has to do with real love. In the mass media, the usual presentation is that you go to Venice or Paris, look into someone's eyes, and fall in love just as you might fall into a manhole. I can't imagine how such a notion of love got started. Real love is the result of a lot of hard work over a long period of time. It is developed through trust and loyalty and patience, learning not to say a harsh word or even show disrespect when we are provoked.

Over many years this kind of love can grow to such an extent that those you love will *know* you are incapable of hurting them, whatever lapses they may have. Imagine the security this brings! Your trust and loyalty can go so deep that you never even have a divisive thought.

This applies not only to one relationship but to all. When we have totally forgotten our own pleasure and convenience in seeking the welfare of others, the wall of our separate ego has broken down. When we see others happy, we feel happy; when we see others suffering, we try to help. There is no individual burden of sorrow that we must bear alone.

This is what is meant by seeing the underlying unity of life. It is not an intellectual abstraction but a living experience, in which we see the Lord everywhere, in everyone, all the time.

The Destroyer

This name is a stark contrast with the usual image of a loving Lord. The orthodox explanation is that it refers to the apocalypse. The Hindu view of the creation fits well with contemporary cosmology: the universe is said to explode into being, along with space and time, from a state of pure potentiality, and to expand for billions of years. Then it is withdrawn into a state of potentiality again. That which was before the creation of the cosmos and will remain after its dissolution, changeless and unchangeable, is the Lord.

Yet there is also a personal application of this name, which is often misunderstood by scholars: when we have done everything we can to reduce the selfishness and self-will that stand between us and the Lord, it is the Lord himself who finally destroys our sense of a separate, selfish personality, releasing us from separateness into the unitive state. At that time we will see that even in trying to go against our selfish impulses, it is the Lord, the Self, who gives the motivation. The desire to go against selfish desire is one of the surest signs of spiritual progress, and it has to come from a source far deeper than the petty ego from which self-centered desires spring.

One of the best ways to do this, particularly with people we have to rub shoulders with frequently, is to practice patience. Patience, such a quiet skill, can actually dissolve self-will—and like physical endurance, it grows through practice. To speak gently, to act kindly at precisely that moment when we long to lash back, is the surest way of developing patience. When somebody who meditates comes to me with a sad tale of how he has been wronged, I often want to beam and exclaim, "What an opportunity! This is your chance to break through to a deeper level in meditation."

Increasing patience puts an end to many emotional problems, even some that have been victimizing us for years. Surprisingly, it may even put an end to physical problems, particularly those that are aggravated by stress, competitiveness, and compulsive hurry. Of course, we have to observe the basic rules of right living, both physically and emotionally; patience cannot make up for lack of vitamin B-12. But we will be amazed at how good patience makes us feel, and how much better we are able to work with people who used to provoke psychoallergies. The benefits are so compelling that once you see this, you may actually start asking the Lord to provide you with more opportunities to practice patience and make it grow. "I can take it," you hear yourself promising. "Right on the chin." That is the stuff of which budding mystics are made.

When this happens, you begin to see why great mystics speak so gratefully of trials and tribulations. They are not being perverse. Like an athlete who accepts a grueling training regimen because she knows it will stretch her physical capabilities, the mystics accept hardship because they know from experience that trials draw out their best. I think Mahatma Gandhi actually used to feel uneasy when things were going too well for him. He knew—and so did his opponents—that he was at his best when life was raining blows on him. In a similar spirit, a few lines from Teresa of Avila give a great lover's response to times of trial:

> When that tender hunter from paradise
> Released his arrow at me,
> My wounded soul collapsed
> In his loving arms.

My Beloved has become mine
And without a doubt I am His at last.

He pierced my heart with his arrow of love
And made me one with the Lord who made me.
His is the only love I have,
And my life is so transformed
That my Beloved has become mine
And without a doubt I am his at last.

When life is difficult, it can strengthen us greatly to remember this image of the "tender hunter" who strikes us, as John of the Cross says, with the "wound that wounds to heal." Giving up selfish habits, going against self-will, learning to forget ourselves by putting others first—all these can hurt a good deal. What Teresa is implying is that if we are not willing to be subjected to this kind of pain, we might as well forget about becoming one with the Lord. So far as I know, there is not a single mystic who does not talk about the difficulty of it, the distress. The Lord can be quite tough. He says, "I am going to put an arrow straight through Teresa's heart, so that it comes out the other side and sticks in that tree. If she can't take it, she can continue to be separate." If we want to be able to love anyone at all, we have to overcome the very human tendencies to blame, manipulate, and turn resentful.

There is pain in this, but after the pain—even mixed with it, when we understand what is taking place in our hearts—there is joy, the exhilaration of freedom. Releasing ourselves from the tyranny of selfish habits means releasing our hearts and minds from bitter hostilities, from jealousies, from burning desires we cannot control. So mystics like Teresa confide to us, "It was a great day when this divine hunter got me in his sights." We read accounts of their lives and we think, "How tragic! They turned their back on so many good things." Yet here is Teresa telling us that those were the happiest moments of her life. For as she fell, wounded, the Lord's loving arms were there to catch her; she fell from separateness into the unitive state.

He Who Is Invoked
in the Act of Sacrifice

This name hides a minor mystery. *Vashatkara* means "he who is invoked by the sacred word *vashat,*" which is ice cream to Sanskrit scholars. This ancient word is exclaimed in a particular ritual at the moment when an offering to the Lord is poured onto the sacrificial fire.

Shankara, the great mystic of medieval India whose authority is unassailable on spiritual matters, says that *vashat* is simply a mantram, like the sacred syllable *Om.* But it may be given a more practical interpretation, for all of us are expected to make our lives an offering to the Lord, from whom life came. In practical terms, this has very little to do with rituals and formal worship. Making our lives an offering to the Lord means putting others first, living for the welfare of the whole rather than just for ourselves, for the Lord is present in all.

Abundant

When you take something from infinity, infinity remains. Similarly, you can take all you can hold of the Lord's qualities and there will always be more. The measure of what we can take from him is what we ourselves can carry. If we go to him with a narrow heart, he will not be able to put much love or patience in. But great mystics like Saint Teresa or Mahatma Gandhi, who have emptied themselves of themselves, are not only full of the Lord but are open conduits for his love. They have burst ordinary human limitations; their resources are endless. The more they give, the more they have to give; the more they love, the more they are able to love.

Not only can you not exhaust such people, you find that they have given you so much patience that you too can pass it around a little more. "Here, Marilyn," they say, "let me give you a basketful of patience." "Hey, Rhett, you take two." They go about distributing patience and their reservoir of love remains full. Even ordinary people like us will find that the more we keep on giving such gifts, the more we have to give. We are drawing on the fullness of the Lord, who is right within.

Intellectually, this idea may be difficult to understand. The problem is our idea of the human being. We think we are very limited creatures, very small, good for maybe only fifteen minutes of love or patience before we have to crack. Instead of identifying with our deepest Self, we are identifying with some biochemical-mental organism. I don't spend much time trying to reason with this idea. I just say meditate, repeat your mantram whenever you can, and try it for yourself: see how far you can stretch your patience.

Of course, there will be lapses. But after a while you will see for yourself how comfortable you feel with everybody, how secure you feel wherever you go. You will find that when you have to go into difficult situations, you will do so with a quiet sense of being equal to the challenge. You know you can listen to criticism calmly, keep your temper, and make your point with kindness and humor; and you know that by and large, other people will respond.

These are tremendous discoveries, which give only a hint of the heights to which a human being can rise. Once we see this for ourselves, we will catch the exhilaration of the mystics when they say that because the Lord is our real Self, there is no limit to the height to which we can grow.

Water Lily

KUMUDA

Among these lofty appellations, we also get some familiar names that celebrate the beauty of the Lord, which love of him awakens in our heart.

Some of the most appealing of such names refer to flowers, which make favorite names for girls in India. In central India, where the university draws students from every part of the country, my roll books carried regular garlands of tropical names. *Kumuda,* for example, is a lovely kind of water lily that the poets say blooms at night when the moon comes up. With such romantic associations, you can see why a girl named Kumuda would be faced with great expectations when she showed up as a freshman on a college campus.

The Lord too is called Kumuda, and the application is that just as this beautiful lily waits for the moon to rise, our heart is waiting for the love of the Lord to open it like a bud. When love of him begins to flood our heart, no discourteous word can come out of our mouth, no unkind act sully our hands, no jealous thought arise in our mind. This is when the human personality blossoms into full beauty.

When the lotus blooms, it doesn't need an advertising agency to generate name recognition. No one can keep away. Similarly, when you do your best to put other people first, even if it means ignoring your own private satisfactions, everybody enjoys being around you.

Jasmine

KUNDARA

This is another name rich in associations. When I was
teaching English at a college in central India, I remember,
men leaving campus at the end of the day used to stop by
the flower stand for garlands of jasmine to take home to
the ladies in the family. Half a rupee then would buy a
couple of feet of delicate petals with a haunting perfume.

Walking into my classes in those days was like entering
a fragrant garden, so many girls had twisted garlands of
ivory jasmine in their shining black hair. Some would do
their hair in a style you may have seen in the frescoes
from the Ajanta caves, with a bun on top, pulled a little to
one side, and a garland woven around. Others had a little
chignon at the back. But most simply twisted strings of
blossoms into their long, thick braids. And even after the
flowers had faded and been tossed away, the girls' hair
would still be fragrant with the scent of jasmine. Certain
boys used to sit at the back of class, sniff audibly, and
heave great sighs of appreciation.

Lovely flowers smell sweet, the Buddha says, but they
fade, and their fragrance cannot last. The fragrance of
goodness abides. When you have been in the presence of
someone who has realized the Lord, you will take home
with you a little of that person's kindness and patience, a
heart at peace, just as the smell of roses remains in a room
long after the flowers are gone. Even you and I, when we
can forgive unkind words or malicious behavior and not

carry agitation in our hearts, will leave a fragrance that others too will carry away.

What is the appeal of calling an expensive perfume My Sin? "My Forgiveness" would be so much more alluring. Instead of Evening in Paris, this is evening in paradise. When you live with someone who can forgive from the depths of his heart, you are living in heaven here on earth.

He Who Wears
Garlands of Forest Flowers

VANAMALI

Krishna is often portrayed as a young man with a garland of wild flowers, the delicate blooms of the forest, around his neck. It's not a sophisticated corsage from the florist's shop; everything is natural, naturally beautiful.

Garlands, called *malas*, are very popular in India, and Indian poets have always been fond of the imagery of flowers. Mira, one of the most beloved saints of medieval India, tells Krishna in a song, "I am going to wear you like a flower in my hair, like earrings in my ears, like a garland around my neck, so that I remember you always." That is the purpose of the *Thousand Names*. If we remember who is the source of all beauty, all plants will remind us of the Lord.

Houseplants are everywhere today; people have African violets on their desks at work, ferns on the stereo, fig trees in the living room corner. In some places it is fashionable to tear down a wall or open up a window and attach a miniature greenhouse. Berkeley, where I used to live, had a store called Plant Parenthood. Why not do the same with patience and forgiveness? We can surround ourselves with compassion, open up our lives to goodwill. All these flourish with just a little care. When you fly off to Iceland on a tour, don't you ask your neighbor to take care of your African violets—spray them, chat with them, pick off the bugs? Some people spend an hour or more a day with this kind of thing. With the same attention, houseplants like love and tenderness will blossom in your life year round.

Sri Krishna's garland of wildflowers is always fresh from the forest. When you or I receive flowers on a special occasion, we have difficulty keeping them fresh, but Krishna's garland never seems to fade. The Hindu scriptures say that this is a sure giveaway of a divine being. If you ever meet anyone whose corsage or buttonhole bloom never wilts, be alerted: this is no ordinary Joe or Jane!

The Uplifter

The Lord is infinitely tender, but we should never forget his toughness. He and he alone has the strength to lift us out of trouble and despair, and ultimately out of the sea of birth and death.

When I go to the beach for a walk, I sometimes see a Coast Guard helicopter flying perilously low, on a mission of mercy to rescue someone in trouble at sea. This is how I picture Krishna. No matter how close we are to drowning in the sea of selfish conditioning, if we can reach into our deeper consciousness through meditation and the Holy Name, the Lord will act as our internal helicopter. His promise is given in the Bhagavad Gita:

> But they for whom I am the goal supreme,
> Who do all things renouncing self for me,
> These will I swiftly rescue from the fragment's cycle
> Of birth and death to fullness of eternal life in me.

When we get in trouble, repeating the name of the Lord can pull us out; but that in itself is not enough. If, in spite of our best efforts, we accidentally fall into waters that are over our head—for example, if we get into a situation where a strong desire can sweep us away—then repeating the Holy Name can release the will we need to get ourselves out. This help comes from a depth beyond our ordinary reach, which is what the great mystics mean when they say the Lord came to their rescue. But after that we are on our own again. The Lord expects us to

76

learn from our mistakes. If we go on jumping in over our heads and then calling out, "Save me!" he will simply reply, "You'd better save yourself. That's the only way you'll learn."

All-knowing

I remember once seeing a clever British film dedicated to
"all those who got away with it." As far as real life is
concerned, I don't think anybody gets away with anything. The Lord is within us; what can we hide from
him?

Inside each of us, my grandmother used to remind me,
is a perpetual Peeping Tom with his eye right to the
keyhole of the mind. Every thought is registered. It took
me years to be able to swallow this concept, which
seemed preposterous to me as a child. Today, realizing
that the Lord is not outside but our real Self, I see how
remembrance of him can really keep us on our toes.

One of the fascinations about detective novels and spy
stories seems to be the idea of tracking people down.
After you finish reading one, you may find yourself
thinking up ingenious ways of covering your tracks. It
might seem simple. But even though there is no hidden
camera focusing on you, no long-range mike, no secret
agent to bug the olives in your salad, someone inside is
tuned in to everything that goes on in your heart.

The Lord does this not to torment us but to protect us.
Doubts, depressions, and pangs of guilt are really an
extremely sophisticated alarm system installed in every
nerve and cell of our being, warning us when the things
we say or do or think run counter to the laws of life.
Blaming circumstances or other people in such cases is
ignoring the real culprit in the story. When we repeat the

mantram we are praying, "Lord, I know I have wrong thoughts. I know I sometimes say or do harmful things. Please help me to turn wrong thoughts into right ones, and to remember that you live in me and in everyone around me."

He Who Never Sleeps

NILA

In India we have a great festival called Shivaratri, the Night of Shiva, which devotees celebrate by repeating the mantram and worshipping the Lord in various other ways from dusk until dawn. It is like saying, "Lord, you stay awake all year long to keep us out of trouble. So tonight *we* will stay awake, chanting your name throughout the night, so you can get a good night's sleep."

This is a real measure of love, because sleep is one of the human being's favorite pastimes. After a couple of nights without sleep, people can try to tempt you with anything on the face of the earth; you will just yawn and say, "Ask me again after I wake up." You won't want anything except a nap. If Romeo's friends had kept him awake just one more day and night before that fateful glimpse of Juliet, he might have got as far as "It is the east!" and forgotten all about the sun of his delight looking down on him from her window. He might have nodded off instead of climbing up onto that balcony, and saved both of them a good deal of trouble. That is the principle behind the overnight vigil, practiced in all monastic traditions to keep physical passions at bay.

If you can fall asleep in the mantram, however, you do not have to express your love for the Lord by keeping vigil; you can express it while you sleep. "You've been on duty all day long," you assure him. "Now let your name protect me during the night. With it at work in my consciousness, you don't have to be watchful; you can go ahead and get some sleep." The secret is that if we fall asleep in the mantram, it will keep on repeating itself until we wake up: a constant, comforting reminder that will calm the mind, banish conflicts, and leave us refreshed and restored when morning comes.

Whose Face
Is Everywhere

SARVATO-MUKHA

If you want to see God, the mystics say, you have only to look around you. Everyone's eyes are his eyes; every face reflects his.

This is not an intellectual understanding. When you realize the Lord in your own heart, that is how you will actually see. The English mystic Thomas Traherne has a beautiful passage describing how the faces and figures around him were transfigured by this vision:

> . . . young men [seemed] glittering and sparkling angels, and maids strange seraphic pieces of life and beauty! Boys and girls tumbling in the street, and playing, were moving jewels. I knew not that they were born or should die; but all things abided eternally as they were in their proper places. Eternity was manifest in the light of the day, and something infinite behind everything appeared. . . .

Rosy-eyed

LOHIT-AKSHA

Sri Krishna's eyes are considered particularly beautiful, and they are often compared with the loveliest of flowers, the lotus. When the lotus blooms early morning, the rays of sunlight pass right through the translucent red petals, turning each flower into an exquisite goblet filled with liquid light. When you look at someone with love, this name reminds us, the melting light of the Lord will shine through your eyes, filling them with his glow.

According to yoga psychology, there is immense power in our human passions. As that power is transformed into love, the light released cannot help shining in our eyes. That serenity, that luminosity, is a kind of liquid effulgence that comes not from us but from the Self within.

The Supreme Blessing

MANGALAM PARAM

This word *mangala* is an auspicious one in India; it is repeated many times at a wedding. *Mangalam* means blessing, it means joy, it means purity, it means love. In South Indian concerts, the last piece is always *mangalam*: a prayer for the Lord to give his blessing to performers and audience alike.

The Lord is supreme joy and supreme love; he is the supreme blessing our life can receive. In seeking him through meditation and serving him in those around us, repeating his name with devotion and dedication, we are slowly making ourselves ready to receive this great blessing, the precious legacy of unity that is buried deep within us. For our real nature is none other than joy, none other than love.

The Self in All

The Lord is present not only in those we like and who like us. He is present equally in those we do not like and who dislike us. He lives in all, and when we attain spiritual awareness we will see him in all, whether they are for us or against us, whether or not they belong to our race, sex, country, or religion.

To begin to see like this, we must learn to overcome our likes and dislikes. It is only natural to like those who like you, and to return dislike with dislike. We need a certain degree of detachment to be able to get along with people who are difficult—detachment not from them but from our own opinions and self-will.

In English the word *detachment* sounds negative; people usually associate it with indifference. Actually it is attachment to ourselves that makes us indifferent to others. What life requires is detachment from ourselves, which opens the door to sympathy, understanding, and compassion.

Detachment is the key to effective action. As long as we are driven by selfish concerns, we can never see a situation clearly, which means that we cannot act appropriately either. People driven by the desire for fame or power, for example, cannot help manipulating those around them. Gradually they lose respect for everyone, including themselves. They end up estranged from those around them, and the little empire they have built up becomes a source of sorrow.

Lack of detachment, however, is not limited to those who are greedy for their own ends. Many good causes have failed because those who supported them lacked the detachment to see when they were defeating the very purpose for which they were working.

To take just one example, some of the peace demonstrations I used to see in Berkeley were not exactly peaceful. I remember once being amazed to see a student forget himself so completely that he was threatening someone with a big sign saying "Peace Now." This is just the kind of mistake all of us make when we get so wrapped up in our own way of thinking that we cannot see anything clearly.

Some time ago, while my wife was in the bank, I decided to stay in the car and read the paper. The door of the car was open, and a dog, rather plebeian, came up and looked at me for a long time to see if I was worth cultivating. He must have decided I was, because he put two paws on my lap and said, "Bow-wow." I said, "Yes, thank you, I am always well." He had quite a nice way about him, so he probably would have understood if I had said instead, "I don't have time to talk to dogs"; I imagine he would have just said, "I feel sorry for you," and walked away. But I can understand the ways of dogs easily, and I started petting him. By this time he was drawing himself more and more into the car until at last more of him was in than out. He was sitting on my lap and we were getting along very well when a lady who was passing by said jocularly, "He's a mutt. He likes everybody."

Mutt or not, I wanted to tell her, that dog was teaching us a lesson. Those who like everybody, even if their opinions or color or social status is different, have tremendous potential. Such people can go far spiritually, because they identify themselves very little with their body, feelings, and opinions. They do not forget that people are people just like them, so they do not put labels on them: "reactionary or radical," "straight or not so straight," "for me or against me." And they never make the mistake of thinking of people as political animals or economic units; for all of us have feelings that can be hurt and needs that should be respected. When you see someone like this, remind yourself that he or she has already some awareness that all of us are one. That is what detachment means.

Without detachment, however, we cannot help being rigid in our attitudes and opinions. Times change, the needs of society change, but those who lack detachment will find it impossible to adjust their views.

Mahatma Gandhi provides the perfect example of someone who was never afraid to change an opinion. Most people remember Gandhi as the man who led India to independence from British dominion without ever resorting to violence. But in his earlier days he supported the British Empire, and even went so far as to recruit an ambulance corps for the British army in the First World War. When asked about these inconsistencies later, he used to reply simply, "That was how I saw things then." No defensiveness, no apologies. He had learned to identify himself not with his attitudes or opinions but with the Self. When we have this kind of detachment, it can save us a great deal of wasted turmoil over opinions we may have held or mistakes we may have committed in the past.

That

If you ever find yourself in a dilemma over whether to call the Lord "he" or "she," you can always get out of it by saying "That," which is a word without any gender at all. Tat is neither he nor she; it simply points.

Gender is a property of the body, which is a very temporary affair. The supreme reality, your real Self and mine, has no sex. It is masculine and feminine together, and at the same time it is beyond both. When we worship God as Father or Mother or Beloved, we are simply wrapping reality in a particular form that speaks to our love and longing. It may not be logically defensible, but logic is not what moves our lives.

In the Upanishads we find the great statement *Tat tvam asi,* "You are that": that subtle essence of all things, that supreme being in the depths of consciousness. Entering these depths in meditation, in fact, is the only way this reality can be known. It cannot be expressed in words. As the Taittiriya Upanishad says, "Words and thoughts turn back, unable to attain That." Words cannot even get close to that door. Thoughts get farther, try to walk through, but then the mind becomes completely still and thoughts disappear.

Sri Ramakrishna used to illustrate this with a marvelous story about a doll made of salt. The doll went to measure the depth of the sea, but as soon as it entered the water it dissolved and became one with the sea. This is what happens in *samadhi,* the final union with the Lord that is the culmination of all spiritual effort. When the senses are stilled, when the mind is still, when the intellect does not waver, that is the supreme state called yoga or samadhi. Then we see the vision of God, the "face behind all faces," and we know beyond doubt that we live in God and that he lives in us.

In that state, the little "I" that we identify with today is no longer there; so the Self can shine forth in full glory. After samadhi, we keep what Ramakrishna called a "ripe I"—ripe like a fruit that barely stays attached to the tree. That trace sense of "I" is necessary for relating to others with love and compassion; without it, the unitive state can be rather impersonal. But the "ripe I" never really believes itself to be separate from the rest of life, so it can do no harm.

Who Has No Form

This is a rather strange-sounding name for a deity, but the supreme reality has no form. In our modern civilization, with its constant emphasis on the physical, it is difficult for us to imagine even for a moment that we are not physical creatures. But our real Self is not material; it can have no shape.

At the same time, we should never forget that the same reality takes various forms in the eyes of its devotees. Mira, our beloved medieval saint and poet, looks at the Godhead and her loving heart sees Krishna; Saint Teresa of Avila looks at the same Godhead and sees Christ. Both see truly, yet no one can ever see the whole truth: God is formless and has taken infinite forms as well; he is above all distinctions of form and formlessness too.

Here is Sri Ramakrishna's reply to the question of whether God has form or not:

> Think of God as a shoreless ocean. Through the cooling influence, as it were, of the devotee's love, the water has frozen at places into blocks of ice. In other words, God assumes various forms for his lovers and reveals himself to them as a Person. But with the rising of the sun of knowledge, the blocks of ice melt. Then one doesn't feel any more that God is a Person, nor does one see God's forms.

The Immortal Craftsman

TVASHTA

This is one of the Lord's more obscure names, but it has a good pedigree: it dates back to the Vedas, India's most ancient scriptures, which in their oral form may date back five thousand years. In the Vedas, Tvashta is a sort of divine craftsman who makes all kinds of wonderful things, especially tools, for the gods. He is also a great builder.

Recently I went to attend the housewarming of a good friend of ours, whose unusual new house other friends had helped to build. I felt pleased to say, "Yes, it was Victor who built all those cabinets; Jeff won some kind of award for the design." But imagine if I had tried to maintain that that house was not built by anyone in particular; it just happened. Some tremendous storm must have felled the trees, and by curious accident lightning split them into two-by-fours. Then a great earthquake might have shaken the timbers together into the form of a house. "Powerful coincidence." The house was built not by design but by a wonderful coming together of various forces.

This sounds silly, of course, yet it is not that different from the language of some scientific accounts of creation. When I hear someone say, "Oh, there is no 'supreme reality'; there is no one responsible for this universe," I feel a little amused. The Lord is the architect, the builder, and the building too—but not some cosmic being outside it all; he designs and builds and guides from within. This point of view is quite tenable on scientific terms, and in fact physics and cosmology today have taken on a tone of awe in the face of the mysteries of creation.

Free from Sorrow

ANAGHA

Sanskrit often describes perfection by saying what a thing is *not,* the way English uses words like "flawless." This is especially useful when talking about the supreme reality, which is beyond description. The Upanishads use the formula *neti, neti,* "not this, not that," to remind us that anything within mundane experience falls far short of the divine.

Anagha, "without sorrow or evil," is one such name, negative in form but wholly positive in meaning. Human experience is often touched by sorrow, but union with the Lord means direct experience of a state of mind beyond all personal suffering. This does not mean that the man or woman who has realized God never knows pain. To realize God is to see yourself in all creatures, which means that you feel their sorrows as your own. But you no longer grieve over any problems of your own, and beneath everything else there flows through consciousness a permanent current of joy which sustains you in the face of pain and tragedy.

"A certain amount of pain in life is unavoidable," my grandmother used to tell me, "but why bring in any that you can avoid?" Whenever she said things like this, I knew she was talking from personal experience, and I believed her. Yet for a long time I had difficulty putting this faith into practice.

On the physical level it is easy to understand when someone gives us directions in life. If I tell you that you

93

can get to the bank by going down this road and turning right, you wouldn't turn left; nobody would. But when the scriptures say, "Don't take that road; it won't take you to the bank but to bankruptcy," we often can't seem to understand. Pain, sorrow, and suffering are often guideposts on the road of life, reminding us that the road we have chosen is not taking us where we want to go.

All religions tell us not to follow self-will, the seductive road of strictly private satisfaction. But often what we desire covers our eyes and plugs our ears; we cannot understand. Then the suffering that self-will entails can act like a highway warning sign—"Turn Back! Wrong Way"— prompting us back to the road that leads to the end of sorrow.

He Who Nips
Wrong Actions
in the Bud

DUSHKRITI-HA

Dushkriti is "wrong actions," from the same root as the word *karma*. As the Compassionate Buddha says succinctly, we get in life what we work for. If we ride roughshod over other people's feelings, for example, we are bound to alienate those we live and work with, which means that after a while they are likely to start riding roughshod over us. There is nothing unfair about the law of karma, and no outside agent is required. We reap just what we sow.

Help comes when we ask the Lord—our real Self—from the bottom of our heart, "I am a victim of my own habits; I want to change, but I've been conditioned to act this way all my life. What can I do to save myself from the bad karma I have been accumulating?" The answer the Gita gives is that our selfish conditioning begins to fall away when we learn to put others first and to return sympathy for resentment and love for hatred. Putting others first quickly dissolves the conditioning of selfish habits, even if they have been entrenched for many years. When we can do this, it means we are learning the lesson which our bad karma had to teach. The purpose of karma is not punitive; it is educational. When we forget ourselves completely in love of the Lord, the nexus with karma is cut. That is why Sri Krishna assures us in the Gita:

> Be aware of me always, adore me,
> Make every act an offering to me,

And you shall come to me. This I promise,
For you are dear to me.
Abandon all supports, and look to me alone
For protection. I will purify you
Of the sins of the past; do not grieve.

The Purifier

PAVANA

Just as sunlight purifies running water, the name of the Lord purifies the mind. When you drink polluted water, you are liable to develop ailments from dysentery to heavy metal poisoning. People are beginning to wake up to the danger this problem poses to the whole globe, but almost nobody seems to be aware that a polluted mental environment can cause even greater disasters. When we don't take the trouble to purify our own mind—and, I might add, the mental environment of our society— infective agents like anger, hostility, lust, and greed can spread before we realize what is happening.

Thought-infection is passed by the way we act and the way we speak, and nothing spreads it faster than the mass media. Our magazines and movies, our radio and tele- vision shows and popular music, are an environment almost as pervasive as the air we breathe, and the atti- tudes and ideas with which they saturate us do not often add to the quality of life.

Repeating the Holy Name works like one of those sweepers you see floating in swimming pools, moving slowly around with their long tentacles while they suck up leaves and other debris. We are so mechanically oriented that because the mantram doesn't have tubes and a suction motor, we think it cannot be of much use. But the name of the Lord is a miraculously powerful purifier. If you just keep it circulating around and around, it will clean up the muck of the mind even while you sleep.

We should make use of this potent device on every possible opportunity. While you are riding in a car, waiting in a restaurant, washing dishes, or falling asleep, the Holy Name can be busy. When you are angry, afraid, or caught in an emotional crossfire, you can use its purifying power right on the spot. I can tell you from personal experience that even after repeating the mantram for many years, I still find more opportunities for repeating it. With the mantram, you can use every bit and piece of spare time for spiritual growth.

There is no mystery about this purifying power. The mind has to go on thinking, and what the Buddha calls mental impurities—conditioned trains of thought—are just the mind getting caught in the same thought over and over and over. The mantram breaks up these thoughts and absorbs them, restoring consciousness to a state of calm. If you cannot dwell on anger, for example, it cannot last; the thoughts dissipate and disappear without leaving any emotional residue behind.

Anger *is* dwelling on negative thoughts, nothing more. When we hold a grudge, some part of our mind is repeating over and over a particular incident which infuriated us. We say, "I can't concentrate today," or "I'm having trouble relating to people." The reason is that part of our mind is not there. The Buddha, one of the world's most penetrating psychologists, tells us that whatever we are doing, we should be totally there with a completely one-pointed, wholly integrated mind. When your mind is all in one place, you cannot get frustrated or impatient; you cannot feel restless, inadequate, or afraid.

A fast mind is always divided. So is a mind that is forced to do two or more things at once: as, for example, reading and eating at the same time. And of course the mind is divided when part of it is brooding on the past or future, which happens much more often than we may be aware. Whenever you catch yourself getting speeded up, caught in the past, or doing two things at once, repeat the mantram. That will help you to slow down and do one thing at a time, with all your mind here in the present. This is the capacity of genius, and the secret of being fully, vitally alive.

The Energy of Life

According to the Upanishads, our real Self is covered by five layers of consciousness called *koshas,* which literally means "sheaths." Identifying ourselves with these sheaths is no more accurate than identifying ourselves with a favorite turtleneck or parka.

The outermost kosha is the body, which can be compared to a heavy overcoat that we might wear on a stormy day. This is a clumsy covering which often gets in our way, but after all, it is difficult to function without it. In this context the body is called *annamaya-kosha,* "the jacket made of food." Very precise, very scientific: that is all the body is.

The other four sheaths, roughly speaking, correspond to what we call in English "the mind." One of these in particular gives the significance of this name of God. Just "inside" the body, so to speak, is the sheath that provides the interface between body and mind. It is called *pranamaya-kosha,* "the jacket made of *prana.*"

Prana is energy in its purest, irreducible form; all the kinds of energy that physicists measure, such as light, are particular expressions of prana. In the body, prana is the energy of life, the substrate of all the kinds of energy that sustain the body and mind.

The body, therefore, can be looked on as a container of vital energy, like one of those oxygen cylinders you see at hospitals. Each of us has a built-in prana cylinder, and it is the level of our prana that largely determines the quality of our daily life. This cylinder generally gets depleted as we grow older, but chronological age is not what counts most. When Gandhi was in his seventies he could work fifteen hours a day every day of the week; he needed only a few hours of sleep. At an age when many people worry about balancing their checkbook, Gandhi was able to attend with clarity and compassion to decisions that changed the lives of millions of people—and of course he never even thought of retiring.

Millions of people begin to lose mental and physical faculties when they grow old, not so much because their vital organs are unable to function but because they have run out of gas: prana. You may have a Porsche in excellent condition, but if you don't have any gas in the tank, it cannot run. Prana is the gas that runs this little car that is the body and its engine, the mind, and one of the most important skills anyone can learn is how not to run out of gas.

Essentially this comes down to conservation. There are many ways to conserve prana, and one of the most effective is by training the senses. The five senses—taste, sight, and so on—can be trained just as puppies can, so that when they feel drawn to something we do not approve, we can simply say "Come back" and they will respond. This is not denying the senses, but making them trustworthy servants.

Take the most basic example: food. Many people today are very nutrition-conscious and want to eat only what will make them healthy and strong. So it is very important to train your sense of taste to enjoy what is good for the body and adds to its prana, its vitality, instead of detracting from it. If your taste buds clamor for heavily salted foods with a lot of fat and sugar, you can actually teach them to like good food instead.

To take my own small experience, I was brought up on a very different kind of cuisine in South India, and I must confess to you that Indian food is not always the best; often it is too highly spiced and not very nutritious. Today I eat the very best food in the world. We have our own garden and greenhouse, and we eat garden-fresh vegetables every day. We use little salt, few spices, oil only sparingly, and no sugar to speak of. This is a complete reversal of my likes and dislikes. I have seen Indian friends shudder involuntarily when I describe what I eat; they cannot believe I am still going strong. I just explain, "I have taught my palate to like what I want it to." Taste lies in the mind. To me, my meals taste better than anything I could get in a gourmet restaurant. I enjoy a fresh salad because I know it is good for my body, and because it is prepared for me with loving care.

Eating the right food, then, plays an important role in building up our prana. So does right exercise. I go to the beach every day for a long walk, and it is not just an austere exercise. I enjoy the music of the sea, the roll of the waves, the seagulls flying overhead and the sandpipers scurrying along the curl of the tide. That is what the Buddha would call "right enjoyment": taking pleasure in activities that bring health to the body and peace to the mind.

All of our senses can be trained. It is not just a matter of right food and right exercise. In the Upanishads there is a beautiful prayer, "May my eyes always see what is good. May my ears always hear what is good. May my mouth always speak what is good." We eat not only with the mouth but with all our senses; they are constantly taking in what lies around them, and what they take in, we become.

Just as the body is made of food, the mind is made of the sense impressions it takes in. And just as there is junk food, there are junk experiences and junk thoughts— attractively packaged, but most debilitating for the mind. Training the senses means that we need to be discriminating about what shows we watch, what music we listen to, what kinds of books and magazines we read, what kind of conversation we listen to. Every day the senses give the mind a ten-course dinner, and we can add to our prana, our health and vitality, by not serving it junk thoughts.

Beyond Thought

A great Western mystical document, *The Cloud of Unknowing,* sums up all that really must be said on this subject when it declares, "By love God can be gotten and holden; by thought, never."

In my book of life, love can be learned by anybody. If someone is not able to love, all I say is, "Come and learn." That is the purpose of meditation.

Learning to love requires denying your self-will often, because love means putting the needs of others in your life before your own personal desires. It is not just that we should remember the needs of our family; love is more than just affection for one or two people. Einstein once wrote that only "by widening our circle of compassion" will we find a way out of the violence, mistrust, and exploitation that we see all around us today.

One of the great ironies of life is the fact that to understand love we have to go not to men and women of the world, but to those who have risen above the narrow, possessive relationships we take to be normal. Can the Lord play a bigger joke? It is people like Francis of Assisi and Teresa of Avila who can teach us how to be steadfast in love, how to nurture our compassion so that it can enrich the lives of those around us.

Who Has
All the Weapons
of Battle

SARVA-PRAHARANA-YUDHA

This name is quite a mouthful, but well worth the effort when understood. When we love the Lord with all our heart, he gives us every weapon we need to fight the war within.

Our enemies in this war, the Bhagavad Gita tells us, are ultimately three: anger, fear, and selfish desire. And the most basic of the three is selfish desire, which stands for all compulsive cravings. This is essentially an expression of self-will, the compulsive drive to get what we want whatever it may cost others. Nothing stands between us and the Lord, the mystics say, except selfish desires and self-will.

Compulsive desires are like a net. We are like fish, Sri Ramakrishna used to say, caught in a net of desire, and our driving need is to escape. Unfortunately, we often feel we *like* nets. Yet every time we yield to a compulsive desire, we tighten the net a little more.

Sometimes, when I try to untie my shoelace, I only succeed in knotting it tighter. The more I pull, the more impossible it gets. That is what we are doing when we give in to a sensory urge or self-centered desire. Meditation is the undoing of knots, and indulgence only ties them tighter.

As a boy, if I gave in to a desire when I should have said no, my grandmother would say quietly, "Have you forgotten what happened the last time? Now you have to go through that all over again." Those words always struck a responsive chord. I didn't want to have to go through the same situation and its consequences over and over and over. I didn't want to tie the knot of desire any tighter than it already was.

As Spinoza would say, most people mistake desires to be decisions. The practice of meditation can enable us to have freedom of choice where desires are concerned. To right desires we yield, but wrong desires we resist, generating power that can enrich the immune system.

Protector

RAKSHANA

Life is not given to us for grabbing what we can; it is meant for giving what we can. When we appreciate that this precious human birth has been given to us for making a lasting contribution to the rest of life, we get continuing motivation to keep our mind and body at their best. Nothing can provide a better shield. For some ineluctable reason, life seems to take care of those it cannot afford to lose. Even medically, a growing body of research suggests that living for a purpose greater than oneself probably strengthens the body's healing systems greatly.

Who Enjoys
the Nectar
of Immortality

AMRIT-ASHA

The golden nectar that makes the gods immortal is called *amrita* in Sanskrit. This nectar was churned from the cosmic ocean at the beginning of time. But Krishna doesn't keep this ambrosia all to himself; he wants to share it with us.

The Lord has one great personal desire which haunts him day and night: that you and I should rise above our narrow personal conditioning and be united with him eternally. He is perfect and fulfilled, yet here he is pining away for us, and what do we do but keep him waiting.

Beauty

The syllable *sri* is an extraordinarily auspicious one in the Hindu tradition. When we refer to Krishna we say "Sri Krishna"; when we talk about the Bhagavad Gita, we say "Srimad Bhagavad Gita." Those who attain a high level of spiritual awareness often have *Sri* or *Srimati* attached to their name like this, as a mark of reverence and affection. This is the democratic aspect of mysticism: all of us deserve this title if we grow tall enough to claim our spiritual legacy.

It is not possible to capture all the manifold aspects of our innate glory that this one small word implies. Its root sense is to diffuse light. *Sri* essentially means beauty, not merely physical beauty but spiritual effulgence: "the imprisoned splendor," as Browning says, which shines through the physical form of those whose hearts are pure.

In the Gita, sri is considered a feminine quality. The supreme reality can be regarded as having two aspects, and in Hindu thought the masculine aspect of God is considered passive, never involved in the world. It is the feminine aspect, the creative power of the Lord, that is worshipped as the Divine Mother. The auspicious, benevolent side of this creative power is often called Sri. She is personified as the radiantly lovely consort of Vishnu, shining with precious jewelry and iridescent silks, the abundant bestower of all that the word *sri* stands for:

beauty, prosperity, good fortune, glory, majesty, and protective power.

Growing up in an ancient matrilineal tradition, where women have held land and legal rights for centuries, I absorbed the deeper meaning of this word *sri* very early. My grandmother had lofty standards of what a woman should be, and when a man in our family brought home a bride, Granny would watch her very closely to see her character. It wasn't easy to win praise from her, but two or three times I remember her saying with deep approval, "That girl has sri in her face." You couldn't ask for a higher tribute.

Whenever a man and a woman live together in harmony, cooperating with affection instead of competing, they become established in the permanent romantic relationship represented by *sri*. The question of sexual relations is entirely secondary; what all of us seek is spiritual union. In this supreme secret of sri we will find the fulfillment of all our desires. So *sri* has another connotation: that which is divine.

Ornament

When we follow in the footsteps of the mystics in molding our lives, we add beauty to the world and become an ornament for all. The halo behind the head of the saints is a symbolic depiction of what happens to a person who has lost all selfishness and shines with love for all. It is quite possible for this to happen in our own life. Just as we feel a great thrill on seeing our son or daughter after a long separation, we feel thrilled to see any living creature when we see the Lord within.

One of the phrases that mystifies me today is "the beautiful people." Beautiful people hang out in certain trendy places, drive certain kinds of cars, have certain slightly decadent habits. And, of course, they are young. Those seem to be the primary qualifications. That beauty is limited to a certain age range—say, eighteen to thirty-nine—to say nothing of tying it to the size of one's bank account, is one of the most monstrous superstitions of our times. This is not being beautiful; it is being silly.

Some people today get offended if they can't fool people into thinking that they fit this golden category. If they are forty, they want to look thirty; if their face shows the lines of experience, they may pay thousands of dollars to get the lines erased. This name suggests a very different perspective. If you are forty and have learned something from experience, you are a much greater asset to life than you were when you were a teenager. Your face should show what you have learned; that is what it means to be beautiful at forty.

There is a beauty appropriate to every age, and to try to appropriate the kind of beauty that belongs to a different age is not only unattractive but foolish. "You are wise enough to be fifty-five" should be a thrilling compliment. We can grow in beauty until the last day of our life, and the desire to look on everyone as kith and kin will draw people to us for the beauty of our lives.

Destroyer
of Sorrow

SHOKA-NASHANA

When we are inconsiderate to people, even unwittingly, we are adding to their sorrow. When we refuse to go out of our way to help lift another's burden, their burden becomes that much harder to bear. This is being just the opposite of beautiful. The Lord is not likely to lift a finger to help such people if they turn to him for help; he expects us to draw his help by learning to help others.

When this lesson is learned, however, we begin to see that our own sorrow too is being wiped from the slate of life. When we forget our personal profit and pleasure in living for others, personal sorrow too will be destroyed—not only for the moment, but once and for all.

"I will give you a talisman," promises Mahatma Gandhi: "when you are in doubt or when the self becomes too much with you, try the following expedient. Recall the face of the poorest and the most helpless man whom you have seen and ask yourself if the step you are contemplating is going to be of any use to him. Will he be able to gain anything by it? Will it restore him to a control over his own life and destiny?"

The Poet

Whoever made this world must be a great artist. That is the only reasonable conclusion one can draw from observing the beauty and unity that pervades creation. Go to a fresh produce stand and look at the deep wine-red of the cherries, the rich shades of the peaches, the glow of apples in autumn or of fresh-picked August corn. For those with eyes to see, the plainest wildflower not only shows the handiwork of the Lord, it shines with his very glory. The Lord has said, "I will live in this flower." It may be for only a few days, as in the lilacs outside our kitchen window, but he is there. Wordsworth reflects on how the ocean's sound may be heard in a seashell and declares,

> Even such a shell the universe itself
> Is to the ear of Faith; and there are times,
> I doubt not, when to you it doth impart
> Authentic tidings of invisible things;
> Of ebb and flow, and ever-enduring power;
> And central peace, subsisting at the heart
> Of endless agitation.

In one of her "revelations of divine love," the simple fourteenth-century English mystic Julian of Norwich describes how the Lord

> showed me a little thing, the quantity of an hazel-nut, in the palm of my hand. . . . I looked thereupon with the eye of my understanding, and thought: What may this be? And it was answered generally thus: It is all that is made. I mar-

veled how it might last, for methought it might suddenly have fallen to naught for littleness. And I was answered in my understanding: It lasteth, and ever shall, for that God loveth it.

It is only because we are so preoccupied with ourselves that we do not see the Lord in the commonplace things around us.

"In this little thing," Dame Julian adds significantly,

I saw three properties. The first is that God made it, the second that God loveth it, the third that God keepeth it. But what is to me verily the Maker, the Keeper, and the Lover—I cannot tell; for till I am substantially oned to him, I may never have full rest nor very bliss: that is to say, till I be so fastened to him that there is right nought that is made betwixt my God and me.

Those are very wise words. If we wonder at the beauty of the Lord's creation, how much more wonderful must be the divine source of that beauty, who is beauty infinite.

Holder of the Wheel
of the Cosmos

CHAKRI

In devotional portraits, Vishnu is often represented as
standing casually with one finger of a right hand held up
as if pointing to the sky. On the tip of that finger, perfectly balanced, whirls the disk of the cosmos, called *chakra*
in Sanskrit. As the gospel song puts it, "He's got the
whole world in his hands."

In the *Mahabharata*, Vishnu's disk is referred to by a
name that later passed into Buddhism: *dharma-chakra,* the
wheel of dharma, the supreme law of existence which
holds that all of life is one. Everything in this vast universe of ours is held together in this embrace of unity.

Realizing the divine unity of life brings a state of abiding joy. Most of us have tasted the joy that comes with
loving one or two people. That joy is multiplied a million
times when we love all around us. But this does not mean
we become blind to suffering. As sensitiveness increases,
your awareness of others' sorrow cannot help growing
more acute. Famine in Africa, a ruinous earthquake in
Latin America, war in the Middle East, will not be just
headline stories; they will be tragedies happening to *you,*
to your own family. The millions of children—
thousands of them even in this country, the most affluent
on earth—who do not have enough to eat, who will never
go to school or get medical care or even lead a reasonably
comfortable life, will be always on your mind. But this
awareness is not a burden. It releases compassion, creative resources, and a limitless motivation for doing ev-

erything you can to help, and in that effort to relieve suffering there is more joy than the world knows.

Despite all the media talk of economic strength today, there are ominous signs that even in our United States the proportion of people living in poverty is rising. Tragically, most are women, children, and the aged, just those whom a civilized society would try to protect. Realizing the unity of life means a living awareness every moment that wherever they may live, these are *our* children, our parents and grandparents.

Most of us would feel ashamed to spend our time and money lavishly on trivial pursuits if someone in our own home did not have enough to eat. The mystics would say, "There are millions in your own home who do not have enough to eat. Every minute a child is dying next door." If you want to do something to help, you can begin by not being wasteful of the resources of the earth— its food, air, water, and soil, its trees and fuels. "There is enough on earth for everybody's need," Gandhi said, "but there is not enough for everybody's greed."

All life is part of us. This deepest of convictions can turn the most ordinary human being into a powerful force for unity.

Wielder
of the Mace

GADA-DHARA

In his second hand Vishnu holds a *gada,* a mace or club. This is a not so gentle reminder of the Lord's power, to remind us that he rules us from within. He is the Law-giver and he is the Law.

Many years ago I referred to this supreme law of life in a talk I gave on meditation to some hard-headed Kaiser Aluminum executives in Oakland. After I finished, one of these men came up and said, "You know, we Americans are scientifically minded, and it goes against the grain when you talk about spiritual 'laws.' These are just beliefs, and we Westerners don't necessarily subscribe to them. Shouldn't you say something vaguer, like 'spiritual principles'?"

I motioned him over to a big plate-glass window where we could look down from the Kaiser building onto Lake Merritt, hundreds of feet below. "Would you like to see something spectacular?" I asked. "I'm going to soar out of this window and take a spin around the lake."

"Don't do it!" he said, grabbing my arm in alarm. "Haven't you heard of the law of gravity?"

"I've heard of it," I agreed, "but I don't subscribe to it, so it has no effect on me. After all, it's not a *Hindu* law."

"Whether you believe in it or not," he retorted, "the law of gravity works."

"Similarly," I said, "whether anyone believes in it or not, the law of unity works. If you live in harmony with it, it will support you. But just as with gravity, if you go against it, you have to expect some painful, predictable consequences."

The fact that all of life is one means that everything is interconnected, from the world of things to the worlds of thought. Everything we do or say or even think has consequences, good or bad, according to whether we have acted in harmony with the rest of life or at odds with it. When we act in such a way that others benefit from it, we ourselves reap some of the benefit, for we are part of the whole. But if we do something at cost to others, we reap some of the costs ourselves as well. Put bluntly, selfish behavior has painful consequences: if not immediately, then in the fullness of time.

In our contemporary scientific climate, however, it is worth stressing that this punishment is not meted out by some external Lawgiver. Vishnu, "the all-pervasive," is within us, and when we suffer the consequences of selfish behavior—emotional problems, estrangement, alienation, ill health—we are punishing ourselves. Without this painful aspect of the unity of life, unfortunately, few of us would grow. It is not much of a compliment to human nature, but most of us do not learn from pleasure; we learn from making mistakes and suffering the consequences.

In fairness, the conditioning of pleasure and personal satisfaction is so strong that without making mistakes and learning from them, I think very few human beings can be expected to understand where selfish desires lead. The tragedy is not our making mistakes, but making mistakes without learning from them. Suffering is a simple guidepost on the road of life, meant to keep us from running into a disastrous end.

All religions teach the same lesson: do not follow self-will; it will only lead to sorrow. When we live largely for ourselves, riding roughshod over the feelings of others to get what we want, life itself will ensure that we get increasing insecurity, ill health, and loneliness. There is no other way of awakening our sensitivity. On the other hand, when we open our hearts to the needs of those around us, we get the equivalent of a divine pat on the back: increasing health, vitality, security, and self-respect. As the Buddha might say, we get in life exactly what we work for.

Today, with our psychological orientation, we may want to object, "But that's not fair! We have been conditioned since infancy to try to satisfy personal desires. Do we have to suffer the consequences of unconscious drives over which we have no control?"

Here we see the Lord's infinite compassion. On the one hand, he says, a law is a law. Selfish behavior has to have consequences. We have to understand and accept that, just as when we let go of a ball in midair, we know it has to fall. Yet despite this, we *do* have a choice in how we act; that is what it means to be human. The burden of selfish conditioning, which everyone bears to some measure, begins to fall away when we heed the signposts of suffering and live for others rather than for ourselves. In this way we learn the lesson which suffering has to teach. Once this lesson is learned completely, the Hindu scriptures say, it serves no further purpose. Suffering is an educational tool, a learning device. When we realize the unity of life, personal suffering comes to an end.

Who Carries
a Conch Horn

In his third hand Lord Vishnu holds a conch, which is blown at the time of worship in Hindu temples. Its long, drawn-out cry is a rough reminder of the sound *Aum* or *Om,* referred to in the Upanishads as the cosmic sound. This is not a sound heard by the ear but a transcendent experience of the creative power of the Godhead, of which *Om* is only a limited symbol. Christian mystics too have called this creative power the Logos or divine Word. The Rig Veda says, in terms strikingly echoed by the Gospel According to John: "In the beginning was the Creator, with whom was the Word, and the Word was verily the Supreme."

But the conch has another association also: in ancient India it was blown to rally soldiers to battle. The Bhagavad Gita opens on such a scene, when the "field of righteousness" echoes with the trumpeting of war elephants and the wail of huge conchs from the massed forces of good and evil.

This is a perfect metaphor, for as Gandhi says, this battle takes place inside. The battlefield is each individual heart. In every one of us two forces are at work. One flows toward love, selflessness, happiness, and spiritual fulfillment. The other pulls us back toward our evolutionary past: toward anger, violence, lust, greed, and selfishness.

The force for goodness can never be eradicated, the scriptures tell us; it is the underlying reality of life. So this battle is unavoidable as long as there is selfishness in the mind. We may not be aware of it, but the conflict cannot help going on below the conscious level. Nothing can free us from its stress and turmoil except to face our selfishness squarely and put it to an end.

Bearer of the Lotus

The fourth and last symbol in Vishnu's hands is the lotus. This most beautiful of flowers is the perfect symbol of the feminine aspect of the Lord that we call Lakshmi or Sri. Vishnu and Lakshmi are not two but one, and in most depictions of Vishnu he is accompanied by his consort, "the Lotus Goddess." When Vishnu reclines upon the cosmic serpent Shesha, Lakshmi rests by his side; and when he is born on earth to rescue us, Lakshmi too takes human form to accompany him as his beautiful lady.

There is practical wisdom in these images and stories, for where man and woman live in harmony, the whole family benefits. Man and woman are not made to compete with each other but to complete each other. Vishnu and Lakshmi, the eternal male principle and the eternal female principle, are not really two; they are one and inseparable. This is an urgently practical reminder today, when man and woman are drifting farther and farther apart.

Wherever two people bring out the best in each other, that relationship is blessed by Lakshmi, the goddess of beauty. Beauty will shine from their eyes and in their lives. This is the real secret of beauty, but no one would suspect it from popular culture. Everywhere the message is that beauty is only skin deep and attractiveness a matter of chemistry.

The perfume industry specializes in this kind of propaganda. They come up with such exotic names that I wonder if they take themselves seriously. What is attractive about a name like Obsession? Nothing you can put on your skin can be as alluring as a loving heart and an unselfish mind; these are qualities that entrance everyone. We trust such people and long to spend more time with them. When they go away, as the Buddha says, they leave a fragrance of goodness no one can forget.

Maker & Destroyer
of Fear

Law and compassion, two sides of the Lord, come together in these two names.

On the one hand the Lord is *Bhayakrit*, "maker of fear." As the Bible says, "Fear of the Lord is the beginning of wisdom." Unkind words, unkind thoughts, and of course unkind actions should bring fear to our hearts because they set in motion the law of karma—"As ye sow, so shall ye reap"—to bring that unkindness back to our own doorstep.

But the Lord is also *Bhayanashana*, "the destroyer of fear." If we give him all our love he will remove our fears, because in such love all selfishness is dissolved.

The Upanishads say pithily, "Those who see all creatures in themselves and themselves in all creatures know no fear." The idea that each of us is separate from the rest is the very source of fear. "When there is no other," the Upanishads ask, "with whom can I be angry? Of whom can I be afraid?"

In South India, where I grew up, two things brought fear to almost every heart: snakes and ghosts. Each village had at least one ghost, and Kerala's lush climate is as pleasant for snakes as it is for less fearsome creatures. Some of these snakes are harmless, but several are so poisonous that death can come in minutes. A rationalist might laugh at the fear of ghosts, but I would venture to say that no one from South India, however well educated, walks about in the countryside without the fear of snakes somewhere at the back of his mind.

This danger is especially real at dusk, for that is the time when snakes like to come out and enjoy the evening, just like everybody else, and in the fading sunlight it is difficult to see. At such times anyone can be excused if he suddenly jumps and cries out in fear to avoid what turns out to be only a stick or vine or piece of rope lying beside the path.

Shankara, who came from my same state of Kerala in South India, drew on such experiences to illustrate the nature of separateness and fear. When a villager sees a snake where there is only a rope, superimposing his ideas of snakeness on what he actually perceives, his fright is very real. His heart pounds and adrenaline courses through his body just as if a living cobra lay across his path. What causes that fear? Not a snake, Shankara implies, but the idea of it in the mind.

In just the same way, we often impose our fears on an innocent world. The more separate we feel from the rest of life, the more threatening it seems. Ironically, if we act threatened, we may provoke an aggressive response that seems to confirm our fears. All this falls away as meditation deepens. Your eyes clear, and you see that what you had been afraid of was a projection of your own state of mind.

Answerer of Prayers

One of the most frequent incidents in Hindu mythology is for someone to sit down in profound meditation until the Lord appears to grant a boon. This is a vivid way of reminding us that every strong desire is a prayer. When we have a powerful desire that we can't forget, we are meditating on that desire, actually praying for it to be fulfilled. In time, the very depth of that desire will release the deeper resources to bring it within our reach.

There is nothing occult about this; it is simply the dynamics of desire. When someone is haunted by the desire to make money, for example, that desire focuses all his will and drive and attention. The very intensity of that focus will release creative schemes for extracting wealth in ways the rest of us may never see.

The irony, of course, is that getting your wishes granted is not necessarily the way to become happy. I think the Greeks had a saying that when the gods want to punish us, they grant us our desires. The Buddha would feel quite at home with that statement. We need no god to punish or reward us, he would say; the natural consequences of our actions are their own punishment or reward.

Often we do not realize how our pursuit of personal desires affects other people. We think it's only our own concern. In fact, even desires for little things can have far-reaching effects. From a spiritual perspective, the underlying cause of industrial pollution is desire. Our economy turns out immense quantities of things that are neither useful nor beneficial, for the simple reason that there is money in selling them. Such an economy cannot stop when people have enough; it depends on their feeling that they never have enough. Every day, in the fear that normal human desires might be flagging, many thousands of dollars are spent in whipping up desires for things we may never have heard of, things we may not even know what to do with when they are delivered to our door.

The hazards of pollution, I would say, are part of the stiff penalty we have to pay as a society for letting our desires get out of hand—for what the Pope, in a telling phrase, calls "the frenzy of consumerism." And the responsibility belongs not only to the manufacturers. They only make what they can sell. We do the buying. If we do not buy things we don't need, they will not be produced. That will be bad for big businesses, at least initially, but it will be very good for the health of our children.

The technologists' dream is that someday they will find a way to go on increasing industrial production without such annoying side effects as toxic waste. Either they will discover new ways of mass production that are safe and clean, or they will invent new ways of disposing of byproducts that are hazardous—for example, by shooting them into outer space. Both these sound a little like the age-old desire to get what one wants without paying for it. Even if it could be accomplished, I have trouble imagining an economy that goes on growing endlessly through the increasing consumption of goods and services no one needs.

No technological shortcut is likely to solve the problem of pollution, because the source of the problem is not physical. It lies in our way of living, which in turn reflects our ways of thinking: the desires, aspirations, and values on which we act. If toxic wastes are a problem of overproduction, then I would say the real problem is overconsumption—and to reduce overconsumption, the people to look to are not the politicians or business executives but the consumers themselves, people like you and me.

When I go to a shopping mall, I am astounded to see how many people do not come to get something specific that they need; they come to see what is available that they might want. They walk in asking, "Well, tempt me. I've got time on my hands and money in my pocket; what have you got for me to spend it on?" And the stores reply, "How about a watch that plays video games? A bathroom scale that tells your weight in a simulated human voice? A household robot to serve you breakfast in bed? How about a selection of twenty variations on an unnecessary item which you already have?" Instead of feeling insulted by this kind of approach, we respond in such numbers that new malls spring up every year.

Buying things cannot appease desires. It only feeds the habit of desiring, until we are chronically unable to be satisfied with what we have. Eventually we find ourselves in a state of free-floating frustration, always wanting something more, never content with what we get.

Let me make myself clear: I am not advocating austerity or a poverty-level life style. I am pleading for a middle path between austerity and excess—in a word, for an artistic simplicity, where personal desires are few and a reasonable number of things are sufficient for us to live in comfort, happiness, and good health.

This is not merely a matter of keeping physical possessions to a minimum. What is much more important is keeping personal desires to a minimum, and to a reasonable size. In other words, besides the external environment, we live in an internal environment as well. It is vital to clean up our air and water and soil, but it is just as vital to purify our internal environment, because it is our thoughts and desires that will shape our future actions—not only as individuals, but as a society.

Giver of Wealth

DHANYA

Just as dioxin or vinyl chloride seeps into the soil to pollute water and food, mental toxic wastes like greed, the lust of possession, seep into the mind from our sensory environment and gradually poison our actions. In magazines and newspapers, on television and radio, in popular songs, we are told every day how wonderful life will be when we own certain things or have certain experiences for ourselves.

The desire for wealth is the most obvious kind of greed, and I see it played up everywhere. I think it was G. K. Chesterton who warned that currency is graven images. We haven't lost religion, he says; we have simply substituted money for God. The great banks are cathedrals to money; the stock exchange is a temple. When friends once took me to a brokerage house, the lofty ceilings, hushed tones, and air of reverence made me feel as if I were intruding on a sanctuary. Market quotations flickered across the wall like a continuous prayer, invoking bulls to protect against the bears. When the Dow went up, it lifted worshippers into an exalted state of mind; when it fell, they slipped into depression. In ancient times, devotees inhaled the smoke of burning laurel leaves or drank soma to alter states of consciousness; today we need only a digital display.

The desires of a society are a very important educational influence, more so even than the curricula of its schools. Nobody escapes this influence. It is, perhaps, the primary way in which we raise the next generation. And what are we teaching? To judge from the way we spend our time and money, from what we read and talk about and pay most attention to, an impartial observer from another planet would conclude that the things in life we find most important are pleasure and profit. Few people would come out and say it, and I think few truly desire it, but that is the atmosphere in which our children are growing up.

California, where I live, must be one of the richest states on earth. Around the globe, wherever Hollywood films have gone, it symbolizes plenty. Yet within a few months after the state lottery system was launched, half the people in California had bought tickets. Any elementary school child will tell you that the chances of winning a big prize are less than one in a million. A friend of mine who is a scientist likes to point out that my chances of winning the lottery without a ticket are virtually the same as if I had one. But all over the state people are standing in line for a chance to get rich quick.

My objection to this kind of activity is rather unusual. I don't argue that gambling is sinful, though I do think it is silly. What bothers me is the injection of more toxic wastes—greed—into the mental environment in which we live. I never look at people or events without considering the mental state beneath the surface, and the mental state here is poisonously seductive. With the constant bombardment of the media, you can scarcely go into a store, read a paper or magazine, or turn on the radio or TV for half an hour in California today without having an unctuous voice whisper, "Hello! Wouldn't you like to get a lot of money *free*?"

What we think about constantly, we become; that is the secret of meditation and prayer. Here we are educating people to worship money. When Jesus said long ago, "You cannot worship God and mammon," it was a living warning which we need urgently today, because almost everybody has been caught. It is not for love of money that we should live; it is for love.

Another mental pollutant we might never suspect is a different form of greed: obsession with pleasure. Bumper stickers and T-shirts ask plaintively, "Are We Having Fun Yet?" It seems like such a reasonable demand. We sit by the sidewalk with a little tin can and beg of life, "I don't ask for much. Won't you just drop in a little pleasure for me today, just one thing that I enjoy?" It may not sound very mature, but where is the harm? Doesn't everyone deserve to have fun?

Here let me say quickly that there is nothing wrong in enjoying life's innocent pleasures. Recreation has an important place in spiritual living, as long as it is not at the expense of any creature's welfare—including our own. But again, we should look at the mental state behind those T-shirt slogans, behind the huge surge in revenue to the entertainment, gaming, recreation, and tourist industries. What pollutes the mind is not enjoying life but living for enjoyment, making pleasure a major personal goal. Pleasure pollutes because it focuses us on ourselves. If we had a drug that could extract pleasure and numb us to any pain, which of us would ever grow? Nothing I can imagine could make a person more selfish, less able to deal with the inevitable ups and downs of life and of other people.

I don't think any sensitive person can be satisfied with having fun, no matter how much of it we may cram into our lives. Our need is not for pleasure but for joy—a deep sense of fulfillment that not only never leaves us but actually increases with the passage of time. Fun is living for ourselves; joy comes from living for others, giving our time and love to a purpose greater than ourselves. "This is the true joy in life," George Bernard Shaw proclaims: "the being used for a purpose recognized by yourself as a mighty one; . . . the being a force of Nature instead of a feverish selfish little clod of ailments and grievances complaining that the world will not devote itself to making you happy."

Punishment

Literally this name means something like "the big stick." Suffering is one way the Lord has of rousing the deeper desire for spiritual growth. It chastens us to turn away from selfish pursuits and find joy.

Often it is only when difficulties look insurmountable that we can tap this motivation to probe deeper in consciousness for hidden resources. Every human being has a kind of trust fund in consciousness, like a safe-deposit vault. To claim your trust fund at a bank, you have to establish your identity. There is the same requirement for gaining access to this limitless trust within: you have to establish your real identity. Unfortunately, this means that the false you, the impostor ego, has to go. If you are going to enter this endless vault and walk out with all you can carry, every trace of selfishness has to be removed.

A friend of mine in the old days of British India used to work for an English bank with branches all over the subcontinent. None of the tellers were allowed to leave the premises at the end of the workday until their accounts balanced to the cent. The branch manager, who was British, lived in a suite on the top floor, so he could afford to be strict. If dinnertime arrived before the books were cleared, he could just go upstairs, have a leisurely meal, and come down again in his own good time to see how work was proceeding. On several occasions my friend did not get home until eight or nine o'clock.

Similarly, I would say, our internal accounts should be

balanced every day. Doesn't the Bible tell us, "Let not the sun set on thy wrath"? As much as possible, not only wrath but all the day's emotional residue should be cleared from consciousness before we fall asleep in it, when its poisons will seep into the mind throughout the night and carry over into the next day. I am not saying to avoid agitating situations; learning to face conflict with equanimity is an important part of spiritual growth. But in the evening, the slate should be wiped clean with the mantram and meditation, so you can start the new day with a clear, serene mind.

It is rather ominous for the Lord of Love to be called *Danda,* "the staff of justice," but the name simply reminds us that he makes sure we pay for our wrong actions. It may sound like a dubious name, but with most of us this proves the most effective method of teaching. If we lead a largely selfish life, riding roughshod over people's feelings to get what we want, the Lord must make sure we get increasing insecurity, ill health, and loneliness. That is the only way we are likely to learn sensitivity. On the other hand, when we remember to open our minds to the needs of other people, we get a dose of security, health, and support.

Lord of War

In Hindu mythology, Skanda was a divine child born to command the forces of light and destroy the forces of violence and evil. In the war within, the Lord is our commander in chief, the supreme strategist who can lead us to freedom from selfish compulsions and sorrow.

The problem is that most of us keep this great commander languishing in a back office far from battle. We don't ask him for orders, and if he ventures to point out that his side hasn't been doing well recently, we listen politely and then carry on as before. Nothing can be done in this great conflict until we let the Lord act as our commanding officer. If you have seen old war movies, you can picture him with his chest covered with ribbons and badges and medals, striding into the general's tent at the eleventh hour to take charge. At last he looks up from the battle map and announces, "Colonel, victory is in sight. We move forward at o600." We have to do the fighting; the Lord cannot take our place. But if we let him guide us, he assures us of the courage, the wisdom, and the compassion we need to secure victory if we persevere to the end.

The war within can be thought of in two phases. In the first, our major objective is getting our own fighting forces under control. The second phase, the real battle, is waged against self-will, the fierce demand of the ego to fulfill its desires and have its own way whatever the cost. "Fighting forces" here means our vital energy, which is tied up in the countless desires, drives, urges, and anxieties of the ordinary human personality. The purpose of training the senses, which plays a central role in every major spiritual tradition, is to begin to get this riot of energy in order.

Training begins with teaching our senses to obey us instead of allowing ourselves to be dragged around by their demands. Trained senses are necessary for good health and a long, vigorous life, but the issue is much larger. Those who cannot control their senses are not capable of much depth in their love; consequently their love cannot last.

Most of us have never heard of this idea. We accept the axiom that sensory demands have to be indulged; otherwise, sooner or later, there will be trouble. As a result of this belief, our senses clamor for satisfaction freely, making us miserable until we give in. If we tell them to keep quiet because what they crave is harmful, they pay no attention.

Imagine fighting a battle with five junior officers who followed orders only when they felt like it! At the beginning, getting them to obey is such a fight that they seem more like enemies than allies. But the senses *can* be trained, and well-trained senses make a powerful force for our command.

The Seven-Tongued

Some of the most practical of the Thousand Names are vivid reminders of how vital energy leaks out through the senses. *Saptajihva,* "seven tongues" of flame, refers to the seven centers or planes on which Hindu mystics say consciousness can dwell as *prana,* the creative energy of life. Each of these centers is represented as a little fire along the spinal column, or as a lotus or wheel around a tongue of flame. But they should not be thought of as physical locations; they represent states of consciousness.

The lowest three levels represent the bodily concerns which consume the attention of most human beings: consumption, elimination, and reproduction. Physically these activities actually require very little energy, but because of our emotional entanglement we burn so much of our vitality at these levels that most people live in a chronic energy shortage. The fourth and fifth centers correspond, very roughly, to the mind—the field of emotions—and the faculty of discriminating judgment. The sixth and seventh centers are awakened only on attaining samadhi, Self-realization.

I said that the first campaign in the war within is to train the senses. What this means is learning to free our awareness from compulsive involvement in the lowest three centers of consciousness, where the senses hold sway. When the mind has been elevated to the fourth center, we have scored a great victory. Then senses become faithful allies, and compulsive cravings and urges are left behind.

Until then, however, the senses burn a good deal of the fuel we need for health, vitality, and general well-being. You can imagine your eyes, ears, taste buds, and so on as little ovens. When you go window shopping, vital energy leaps out of your eyes like twin tongues of fire, reaching out for the objects you desire. When you bathe yourself in sensation under a stereo headset, you can imagine flames coming out your ears. Every sensory indulgence consumes prana.

Of course, these ovens have a legitimate function in daily living. But when we keep stoking their fires with sensory offerings, danger is in store. Attention is flowing out without our approval, which is how compulsions are made. Worse, instead of elevating consciousness we are locking it in on the lowest levels of human awareness. This is what is happening when we develop a tendency to overeat, or when we sit in front of the television for hours on end.

To Whom Are Offered
Seven Kinds of Fuel

This is a reference to a very ancient ritual, in which offerings are poured into a sacrificial fire. The symbolism is that the Lord asks us to bring him our selfish desires and throw them into the all-consuming flames of love for him. Passions, sense cravings, and addictions, all our fear, anger, lust, greed, and self-will, can be fuel for this fire. Whenever we go against these compulsions, we are making a precious offering. The Lord does not benefit from these offerings, but we do. Every offering releases energy and feeds the fire of selfless love. When that fire has consumed every selfish preoccupation in the heart, consciousness is unified in love.

The mystics of all the world's great religions, who have risen above private, possessive attachments, teach us how to feed the fire of love until it flames so high that we do not merely love; we become love itself. One Western mystic has called this "love without an object." We need no particular person to love, and no particular reason: we love as the sun shines, and whoever comes into the orbit of that love receives it. "I love because I love," says Saint Bernard; "I love in order that I may love."

Every time we freely give our time, our energy, and our personal resources to work that benefits others, we are making an offering to the Lord. That is the symbolism of the sacrificial fire. If you want to love, the mystics

say, every personal desire, every habit, every private pre-
dilection you give up is fuel for love's fire.

When your longing to love becomes ardent, then, you
begin looking for ways to defy your selfish conditioning,
seeking opportunities for going against your likes and
dislikes if those around you will benefit from it. This
may look perverse, but it is no different from strapping
weights on your wrists and ankles to build up your mus-
cles when you run. Mystics are athletes of the spirit.
When we read about people like Therese of Lisieux or
Mahatma Gandhi going out of their way to do unpleasant things, we should remember they are in training: training for universal love.

There may be no more moving example in the annals
of mysticism than young Francis of Assisi, who was never one for halfway measures. Whether he was pursuing
pleasure or pursuing God, to know was to act; there was
no gap between his understanding and his will.

Shortly before Francis realized that the Lord was calling him, a strange event occurred which prefigured the
stature of the mystic stirring in his heart, ready to burst
out of the confines of Francis's old personality. He had
been fastidious and fun-loving, and though generous to a
fault, he had always hidden himself as much as possible
from anything unlovely or unclean. Particularly revolt-
ing was the sight and even smell of the lepers who occasionally could be seen on the roads around Assisi. On this
occasion Francis was returning from a journey when
suddenly he was accosted by one of these unfortunate
creatures begging alms.

Francis reacted as any of us would have: with an in-
voluntary cry, he leaped back from the disfigured hand
and sunken eyes. His tender heart moved him to toss
some coins—probably, from what we know of Francis
even as a boy, an over-generous amount. But he did so
from a distance, and that old, old revulsion turned his
face away even as he gave.

As he started to hasten away, however, he seems to

have remembered a line of scripture: "Inasmuch as ye did it not to one of these, ye did it not unto me." Before he could have realized what he was doing, in one of those tremendous upheavals of the spirit that marks the greatest mystics, young Francis turned on his heel, ran back to the leper, and kissed him full on the face. And in that instant, his chroniclers tell us, his revulsion turned forever into joy.

Francis, tradition has it, was a small man, but only a great hero can turn suddenly on a powerful compulsion like this and slay it with a stroke. Yet the capacity is latent in us all. The resources are ours; to get access to them, we have only to take orders from the Lord within instead of following the demands of our own ego. "Make me your commander," the Lord tells us, "and I will give you all the weapons you need."

Wielder of the
Bow of Horn

So Vishnu is represented not only with ornaments but
with armaments as well. Just as King Arthur had Excali-
bur, Vishnu has a sword called Nandaka—"that which
brings joy" in battle, for the conquest of selfishness and
separateness brings joy to us and others.

Vishnu also wields a mighty bow called Sharnga, a
symbol of one of the most powerful weapons we can
have in the war within: the mantram. I am not speaking
rhetorically. When you have repeated the name of the
Lord until it becomes part of your consciousness, you
can take it like an arrow, fix it to the bow of concentration, and shoot down any wave of anger or compulsive
desire with precision.

You must recall how William Tell, having got himself
into a dubious situation, managed to hit the apple and not
the apple of his eye. Calling on the Lord with all your
heart can lead to the same skill in dealing with challenges,
for it sends the mantram deep into consciousness to tap
unknown resources.

The mantram has supported me through many grueling ordeals, enabled me to keep my patience and compassion in the face of the fiercest personal attacks. After
many years of ardent repetition it has become the staff of
my life, a constant support which I know I can trust in
any trial.

One of the most effective times to drive the mantram
deeper into consciousness is when falling asleep. Like

meditation, it can help immensely to clear the ledger of the mind for the following day. When you have learned to fall asleep in the mantram, the agitation and even tragedies of the day cannot enter to destroy the peace of sleep. Not only will the mantram protect you from disturbing dreams, it can bring spiritual dreams that strengthen and inspire you, restore your confidence, and prepare you for the challenges of a new day. At the moment that sleep comes, there is an arrow's entry into deeper consciousness. When the last waking thought is the mantram, it slips deep into your mind, where it goes on working and healing throughout the night.

Will

When we hear about the transformation of consciousness, we may feel tempted to object, "You don't know me. You don't know how unpleasant I can be, how incorrigible I am. If you did, you wouldn't be so optimistic. I have made many mistakes, and I am likely to keep on making those mistakes too, because I don't know how to change. In fact, I don't believe it is possible for anyone to change."

This is where the testimony of great spiritual figures down the ages comes in. Again and again they will assure us that they too have made mistakes, sometimes worse than any we may have made. They too have caused trouble to themselves and others. When they tell us that we can remake our personality, they know it is possible because they have done it. By drawing on the power released in meditation, we can gradually remove all the blemishes of self-centered thought and behavior that hide our real Self from view. In order to do this, however, we must put forth a lot of effort, which is the meaning of the name Kratu.

Some time ago I was watching a woodpecker, a creature I hadn't seen since I left India. This woodpecker had a red turban, and while I watched he came and alighted on a huge tree. He was quite a small creature, and the trunk of the tree was enormous. If he had been able to understand me I would have gone up to him and said,

"What, make a hole in that trunk with your tiny little beak? Impossible. Preposterous!"

But this little woodpecker was not intimidated by the size of the trunk. He did not throw up his legs in despair; he settled onto a limb and went about looking for the right spot to begin operations. It is the same way with transforming consciousness; you have to look for the right spot. In some people it is a particular compulsive craving; in some it is jealousy; in some, blind fury; and in some lucky characters, all three. Each person has to look for that spot where urgent work is most needed.

After his reconnaissance, this intrepid creature chose what seemed to me the most solid, unyielding spot and started pecking away rhythmically. He didn't just give a peck or two and then fly off in search of a worm and come back in half an hour; he went on pecking until he was done. I was amazed at his skill. When he had finished, there was such a large hole that if he had gone on, I have no doubt that the entire tree would have fallen. That is the kind of sustained, enthusiastic effort that is required to transform personality.

Unfortunately, this is far from a pleasant process. For a long, long time in meditation, all we are doing is pecking away at what we want to change in ourselves, and there is not much satisfaction in pecking away. At best it is tedious work, and often it is downright painful. As Meister Eckhart puts it, the pauper has to die before the prince can be born. The problem is that all of us identify ourselves with the pauper—the accumulation of habits and opinions, likes and dislikes, which we have developed over the years—and we are not prepared to let him die. We all say, "This is how I am. This is me, for better or for worse."

Here the mystics reply, "This is *not* you. All these quirks are extraneous." In the language of Sufi mysticism, these are the veils hiding the face of the Beloved. We have mistaken the veils for the face, the layers of conditioning for our real Self. Our whole job in life is to remove these veils, to overcome all the compulsive aspects of our surface personality.

One of the most crucial of weapons in the war within is the human will, which is another aspect of this name Kratu. Everything in life, everything in spiritual growth, comes ultimately to strengthening the will until no setback can stop you, no trial or temptation deflect your course.

One of the difficulties that most of us face is that we know where we want to go in life, but we lack the will to take the steps that will get us there. I saw an interesting illustration of this the other day in a rather unlikely place: an article on one of the most spectacular advances in modern medicine, microsurgery. Surgeons are now able to magnify nerves and other tissues forty or fifty times, work on them with diminutive forceps, scalpels, and the like, and sew everything up with invisible thread when they are done, watching their work not directly but on video screens mounted around the surgical theater. They have accomplished miracles. One teenage girl, a promising flautist, had her hand severed in a tragic accident. She was rushed to the hospital where a specially assembled team of microsurgeons actually managed to re-attach her hand. She was discharged within a few months, with every indication that she will be able to continue her musical career.

In us it is often the will that has been severed, cut off from our understanding. This is particularly true in cases of severe addiction, such as to alcohol or drugs. "I don't want to do this," we say, "but I just don't have the willpower." This is not quite true. The will is intact, but it is lying there lifeless. We need a special surgeon to attach it so it can function again.

Unfortunately, no outside specialists are available for this delicate task; we have to do it ourselves. We begin by connecting the will with the tiniest of threads. One way is to say no to some of those innumerable little things that benefit no one: a second piece of pie, a midnight snack, a

TV show you are watching just because it is on. If, on top of this, you can cheerfully give that time to others, your will is strengthened doubly. Not only that, it adds to your capacity to love.

I am not much of an admirer of those who develop a strong will just so they can get what they want out of life. The whole purpose of strengthening the will is to deepen your love. This precious human birth has been given to us not to grab from life but to give to it. When you understand that this is what life is for, you get continuing motivation to keep your body and mind at their best, as instruments of selfless service. As this motivation grows, compulsive habits begin to fall away.

Apart from other things, when we overeat or smoke or drink or indulge in drugs, it shows a lack of love. Everybody can respond to this idea. It is lack of love for others that blinds us and allows us to develop fierce physical and mental addictions. It is love that loosens the bonds of addiction and sets us free.

Without this daily effort at strengthening the will, even little desires can become unmanageable. When a desire outstrips the will, it is a compulsion, which means trouble in every corner of life.

Beautiful

Sri Krishna, the perfect incarnation of Vishnu, is represented as a young man with extraordinary physical beauty. He is thoroughly masculine, yet his thick, long, wavy hair, slim limbs, and delicate features make him as beautiful as a girl. There is even a chic air about him, as if the Changeless were always up with the latest fashions.

One of Sri Krishna's hallmarks is a shimmering peacock feather which he wears in his hair. If you have never seen a peacock dancing, you have missed one of the most magnificent displays of color in nature. I suppose peacocks are not common in the United States, but when one of our small children happened to see a peacock dancing by the side of the road, the hues of his tail glinting and changing in the sun, he got so excited just telling me about it that he almost knocked over the dinner table demonstrating.

The peacock feather makes a perfect symbol for spiritual living. It is the worldly life, the selfish life, that is dull and drab; the spiritual life is full of color. But we have been so conditioned by the glitter of physical attractions that we mistake drabness for color and color for drabness. When we live for ourselves, the Gita says, we are living in the night and calling it day. Sri Krishna's feather is a vivid reminder to wake up.

Krishna is modern enough to be wearing earrings, and his choice of styles would qualify for *Vogue*. But these superbly wrought gold circlets have a fascinating message. If you look closely, you see they are not just rings; they are little crocodiles. "Love the Lord with all your heart," the mystics explain, "and he will come like a crocodile to snap up all your selfishness and swallow your self-will."

I remember reading in the papers that this year's Miss Universe has been crowned. As a former English professor I would like to say, "Let's be precise: Miss *Physical* Universe." I would have no objection to that title; the judges have certain specifications which *are* applicable to physical beauty. But such qualifications have very little to do with real beauty, which abides. I would ask, "May I interview her twenty years later?" In twenty years, you know, going just by physical appearance, Miss Universe might not even get the title of Miss Fifth Avenue. Yet if she is kind, if she is patient, if she can deal lovingly with those who oppose her, I would still count her among the most beautiful women in the world.

The mystics do appreciate physical beauty; I think perhaps no one is more aware of beauty in natural things than those who have realized God. But the immanent, transfiguring beauty they describe in Sri Krishna is not physical; it floods the body from inside. By its very nature, mere physical beauty excites us at first and then soon cloys; it beckons but quickly satiates. Inner beauty— of kindness, of goodness, of patience, of selfless love— may not thrill at the outset; but when you live with someone with these qualities, year after year you will fall more deeply in love. Every minute that you are parted, you will miss that person. Every moment the message of his life will echo in the depths of your consciousness.

The Cowherd Boy

GOVINDA

At this stage of his life, depicted countless times in poetry, art, theater, and dance, Krishna is the cowherd boy Govinda, growing up hidden from the tyrant Kamsa in the quiet village of Vrindavan. He spends his days helping the other boys to tend the village cows in the forests and meadows around the sacred river Yamuna. He carries a flute, whose haunting melodies draw the love of his playmates as the Lord himself draws the human soul, and around his neck he wears garlands of fresh wildflowers. His waistcloth is of burnished yellow silk decorated with delicate borders, so carefully draped that I can almost imagine him fixing it every morning in front of a full-length mirror the way women drape their saris, making sure that every fold and crease is right.

Around his ankles Krishna wears dulcet ankle bells, the kind you may have seen worn by Indian dancers; for he loves to gather the boys and girls of the village on the banks of the river and dance and play his flute on a full-moon night. Everyone in the village loves to hear the delicate tinkle of those anklets, which signal that Krishna is drawing near.

This is a North Indian touch, whose subtlety I never fully appreciated until I taught at a university which drew students from all parts of India. Then for the first time I saw girls wearing anklets with tiny bells. Those delicate sounds had a powerful effect on their male classmates, which seemed to go far beyond music appreciation.

"When you love a girl," one boy in my classes explained, "her anklets sound different from everybody else's. You can tell she is approaching just by the sound." It is the same with Sri Krishna. When you love him with all your heart, the sound of his anklets is the music of the spheres, the universe moving in harmony to the inner ear of those attuned to its unity.

Stealer of Hearts

Picture this enchanting youth playing on his magic flute in the forest setting where he is usually painted, his dark skin set off by the green of thick foliage and the rich blue-black tones of the monsoon clouds, the flowers around his neck lost in the profusion of wildflowers all around, and you will see why Sri Krishna is called *Manohara,* "he who steals our hearts."

Krishna's charm is so irresistible that once upon a time he even captivated Shiva, the cosmic ascetic who is a master of self-control. Shiva and Krishna are different faces of the same Lord, but our mythology has never been intimidated in the slightest by logic or consistency, and Shiva and Vishnu—or Krishna, his incarnation—are sometimes brought on stage together to convey a particular point.

One such occasion was a tug-of-war between the gods and demons at the dawn of time, when both sides struggled to seize the nectar of immortality which had just been churned from the cosmic sea. Krishna, seeing the demons getting the upper hand, made himself into a marvelously lovely woman— Mohini, "she who intoxicates with infatuation"—and strolled casually by, her anklets jingling with her gait. The gods, being gods, kept on pulling, but the demons all looked up and immediately forgot what they were doing. They dropped the rope and sauntered off after Mohini into the forest, and of course the gods grabbed the nectar of immortality and have protected it ever since.

But the story doesn't end there. Mohini, leading this motley procession of demons astray through the forest, happened to pass Lord Shiva where he was meditating. Now, Shiva is probably the most austere figure in Hindu mythology, completely self-controlled. He doesn't spend his days tending cows like Sri Krishna; most of the time he remains in profound absorption, oblivious of the outside world. But Mohini's beauty was so enthralling that even in meditation Lord Shiva finds strange impulses arising in the depths of his consciousness, just as they would have in you and me. He opens his eyes, and when he sees Mohini's alluring form he gets up and starts to follow her. He is just about to throw his arms around her when Mohini turns and whispers, "Hey, take it easy! It's me, Krishna."

That is the appeal of Sri Krishna, who fascinates not only men and women, gods and goddesses, but even the cows he herds every day. When they hear his anklets, these svelte creatures with their lustrous eyes and graceful eyelashes become like devoted little girls. Even the calves, the poets say, stop nursing for a moment and turn their heads up to look at Krishna. You have to have seen a calf nursing to appreciate that; every ounce of its attention is fixed greedily on the udder. Even that passionate attachment dissolves in love for Krishna. When he passes by, the very branches of the trees bend down to touch him and drop flowers in his path, and the Yamuna River begins to sing when he comes to its bank to swim. This is the way the whole of nature looks to those whose hearts are filled with love for the Lord.

In the immemorial mystical tradition of Hinduism, many men and women have had visions of this supreme loveliness in the depths of their consciousness when they attained samadhi. They actually see Sri Krishna, not with physical eyes but with the eye of the soul, and they testify with one voice that he is more real than the separate creatures they see around them with their eyes open.

They are not describing someone outside. Whether we call him Krishna or Christ, Shiva or Buddha or the Divine Mother, this is the glory and beauty of our real Self, who lives in every heart.

This is the very practical purpose of an incarnation of God: that in loving his outward form, as Saint Bernard says, we may slowly be drawn into complete spiritual union. For a great devotee like Mira, Krishna was a living presence every moment; Teresa of Avila found Jesus the constant companion of her soul. In this tremendous romance of spiritual living, the whole of our consciousness becomes flooded with beauty. All conflicts cease; all reservations in our love dissolve. It is in this complete unification of our desires that Sri Krishna reveals his beauty to us, in the thoughts, words, and actions of our daily life.

Charioteer

Rathangapani means literally "he who guides the wheel of the chariot with his hands." In ancient India there were no Thunderbirds, only chariots. The Lord is saying, "Why don't you let me be your chauffeur? Just give me the wheel of your life; I'll drive you to love, to wisdom, to health."

A good deal of shopping around in life amounts to no more than looking for this perfect chauffeur. All kinds of dubious characters—wealth, fame, pleasure—will pop up and say, "You called?" Always ask for their license; and even if they have a clean record, give them a stiff test before handing them the car.

When my wife and I were visiting the city of Madras in South India, we once hailed a taxi to take us round to the reserve bank. The drive took us over an hour. Now, I had some vague reminiscences of Madras from my childhood, and I didn't think the bank was that far. So after we arrived and paid the fee, I checked a map. We were about three blocks from where we had started! The driver had been taking us on the grand tour, all around town.

This is what pleasures do. One comes gliding by and the driver calls out, "Sure, baby! I'll take you right there." We hop in and go round and round and get deposited in the same spot we left off. And the bill! It is only a very rare taxi driver who will take you to your real destination. Sri Krishna tells us: "Find me in your heart, trust me, love me, serve me in everyone, and I'll take you straight to heaven."

Sustainer of Life

JIVANA

The power with which we are able to live is the power of the Lord. No physiology, no CAT scanner, no ultrasound exploration can account for the power that makes your hands move, your tongue speak, your eyes see, your mind think. When we become even vaguely aware of the Lord, we understand that it is his power we are using in everything we do. Then we become very responsible, like trustees of a great treasure. Our life is not ours to use as we like; it is a trust we hold for others.

This is why Mahatma Gandhi says: "I believe that if one man gains spiritually the whole world gains with him, and, if one man falls, the whole world falls to that extent. I do not help opponents without at the same time helping myself and my co-workers."

The Lotus Navel

Some of the loveliest of the Thousand Names evoke the lotus, called *padma* or *aravinda* in Sanskrit, as a symbol of beauty and fertility. Vishnu's consort is often called Padma, the Lotus Goddess. And Vishnu is called *Padmanabha*, "the Lotus Navel," *Aravindaksha*, "the Lotus-eyed," and *Padmagarbha*, "the Lotus Womb"—all references to stories from the rich treasury of mythology with which Hindu children grow up.

One of these stories tells how the universe was born when Vishnu awoke from the long sleep he had been enjoying while floating on the gentle waves of the cosmic ocean. He was reclining upon the great serpent Shesha, just awakening at the beginning of the universal dawn, when a lotus stalk began to grow from his navel. If you have seen a lotus, you may know how it is born on the bottom of a quiet pond and sends up a tender white filament that delicately seeks the surface of the pool, there to blossom into a robust and beautiful flower. In the same way, a mysterious tendril sprouted from Vishnu's navel, gently grew, and eventually produced a magnificent lotus, in the midst of which appeared the god Brahma, the personification of the creative power of the Lord.

Now, Brahma didn't know who he was or how he had come to be seated in the middle of a red lotus blossom, so he looked all around to find out what was going on. That is why Brahma is always shown with four faces, looking north, south, east, and west. But he still didn't know where he had come from. He had been looking all around him for the source of the universe, and of course he could not find it; for the secret of life's riddles can never be found outside.

Finally Brahma figured this out—after all, he is a god. Having searched the universe in all four directions and found no answer to his problem, he began to descend through the stalk of the lotus—a mythic way of symbolizing what happens over many years in the practice of meditation, where we go deep within ourselves to explore our own spiritual roots. He retraced his evolution back down the lotus stalk until at last he reached the source. Then he understood that he springs from Lord Vishnu himself, that he rests in the lotus of Vishnu's being.

Lotus-eyed

One tropically lush spot in my village was the lotus pond near the temple, which was shaded on all sides by stately coconut palms. It was not large, only about the size of a large swimming pool, and at certain times of the year you could hardly see the water because the lotus leaves covered the surface so thickly. These huge leaves are almost as dramatic as the flower. They float gracefully on the water and never get wet, for not even a drop can cling to their lustrous waxy surface. My favorite time to visit that pool was early morning, when the lotuses open their translucent petals to the first rays of the sun and are transformed into cups of light.

This name, one of the most beautiful given to Sri Krishna, compares the Lord's eyes to these delicate, graceful petals full of light. The reason is not just their physical appearance. Their beauty comes from the response they convey, from the depth of compassion he feels for every one of his creatures.

This name can remind us that it is not mascara that makes the eyes beautiful, but tenderness and love. Anyone with peace and love in the heart cannot help having beautiful eyes. Similarly, those who are angry at heart, whatever smooth words they may employ, their eyes will say plainly: "I don't like you. You're not worth listening to." If you want irresistibly beautiful eyes, learn to put others first; think about their welfare and not about your own needs.

It is not only spiritual figures who deliver this message. Albert Einstein once gave the secret of a beautiful life in four plain sentences. "I am happy," he said, "because I want nothing from anyone. And I do not care for money. Decorations, titles, or distinctions mean nothing to me. I do not crave praise." What he is trying to say is that even the thought of wanting to get something from others has disappeared from his mind. Then the only question is, How much can I give? How much can I serve?

The eyes, it is said, are the windows of the soul. When you look at others with love in your heart, it comforts them, strengthens them, makes them feel secure. That is one reason why we respond so deeply to the eyes of those who are illumined, for they have love for everyone. In the Hindu tradition, it is said that there are three ways of communicating spiritual awareness to others—through words, through touch, or through a look. Ramana Maharshi, a great sage from South India who shed his body only a few decades ago, used to sit on his cot in his ashram while people came from all over India just to look at him. He didn't need to talk much. Even Westerners with many questions to ask found that their questions melted away; the look of sympathy, affection, and love in his eyes nourished everyone who came.

Only a great saint can do this. It isn't something that we can pretend to do, or that we can learn in a course at night school; it has to come from a heart full of love and a mind that is completely still. If we could plug up the million and one leakages of our vital energy and rest our mind in peace whenever we liked, that would be a tremendous blessing. But no one can do this without control over the deeper levels of consciousness.

Yet this is something we can all aspire to. We can gradually gain access to these deeper levels by meditating regularly and repeating the mantram as often as possible. It may take many years, but the time will come when you know that in times of trouble—when you are having difficulties with others, or you feel inadequate, or your thoughts are starting to race out of control—the mantram will come to your aid and steady your mind, which is the first step toward stilling it.

Big-eyed

MAHAKSHA

The Lord has big eyes, "the better to see you with." Don't you have an expression, "You can't get away with it"? Millions of good, educated people think yes, you *can* sometimes get away with it. But the truth is that those big, beautiful eyes are always looking everywhere.

At midnight, for example, when everyone is asleep, we ask ourselves, "Who will know if we slip into the kitchen? Who will see if we climb up to the top shelf where that special jar is hiding and steal into those special chocolate chip cookies?" We take one small handful, and nobody is the wiser. "After all," we say, "what they don't know can't hurt."

Nobody has seen except for old Big Eyes, our real Self.

The Witness

SAKSHI

When I was attending my village school, some of us boys—my cousins and a few of our schoolmates—would sometimes rob a nearby mango tree. Of course, we were always absolutely sure that nobody would find out. But I don't think the owner of the tree was quite in the dark, and once, rather exasperated, he went to the extent of complaining to the headmaster of our school. The headmaster became terribly angry. He called all the boys in the class together and interrogated us.

"Raman, did you rob the tree?"

"Yes, sir."

"Is that true, Shankaran?"

"No, sir. I did it, sir."

"Krishnan?"

"I'm the one, sir."

One by one, each boy said he had stolen the mangoes. Our headmaster was quite sure who the real culprits were, but he couldn't get any evidence. Finally, at his wits' end, he told some of the better students, "You boys should at least give a few hints. Why do you all say that you did it?"

We said, "We are protecting the honor of the school." He had to agree with us, and so we managed to escape.

When I got home, however, my grandmother was waiting. Word gets about quickly in a village, and the first thing she said was, "Son, did you steal those mangoes?"

161

I kept quiet.

"Were you in the group?"

I still kept quiet.

"Even if none of you tells anybody else," she said, "there was somebody who saw. Someone inside you is watching everything, someone who never misses a thing."

In the depths of consciousness, beneath the surface of our egocentric personality, dwells the Lord, who is our true Self, ever wakeful, eternally alert. This is the implication of the Sanskrit epithet *sakshi,* "the eternal witness." After we have done something selfish, when we hear a little voice inside saying, "Shabby, shabby, shabby," that is the voice of the Lord within. And when we feel warm inside because we have helped someone, it is the Lord who is making us feel warm.

For the most part, however, we are too absorbed in our personal pursuits to heed these internal cues, and so we are always at odds with our true Self. This is the cause of all the insecurity in our hearts. Somewhere deep down we know the person we want to be, the person who really is within us. But we are so conditioned to look for our satisfaction outside that we ignore this Self, who is waiting so patiently to be found.

Once we make this discovery, we are no longer separate individuals. Our life becomes a lasting, positive force which does not end when the body is shed at death. Francis of Assisi and Mahatma Gandhi are such forces, as alive today as they were when they walked the earth in Italy or India. We may not aspire to become a Francis or a Gandhi, but all of us can aspire to become at least a "mini-force" if we set our hearts and minds to it. The same power which changed the would-be troubador Francis Bernadone into a saint, and the ineffectual lawyer Mohandas Gandhi into a mahatma or "great soul," can enable us, too, to grow to our full height.

Compared to this realization, all the pleasures of life are insignificant. This is the joy we were made for, the joy of coming home to our true Self.

All-Seeing

Because the Lord is the eternal witness, moving to another town or a warmer climate to solve personal problems is not very practical. The video camera is always there within us. The lights are always illuminating the stage, and the tape is endless; it never misses a thing. So the idea that we can really "get away with it" is preposterous.

This is the ancient law of karma, which Jesus stated succinctly: "As ye sow, so shall ye reap." You may not be able to see the connections of cause and effect that operate in your life, but as spiritual awareness grows you will begin to make out a pattern. When you can view yourself with a fair measure of detachment and compassion, you can watch the myriad little incidents of daily life dovetail into a tightly fitting pattern. Until then we cannot see this pattern, because it would throw us into utter turmoil. In his love, the Lord draws a curtain over karmic connections until we have developed the detachment to deal with them.

Once you begin to see this pattern, however, you will understand why you are in a particular situation. If you find yourself being raked over the coals, you will know that it is because you have done a good share of raking yourself. Twenty years ago in Kansas you may have said certain angry words; now you are here in California listening to the same angry words being said to you. You understand, and the turmoil quiets down; you can calmly take the lesson to heart.

This law of cause and effect is accepted as a fact of life by Hindus and Buddhists, as natural as the law of gravitation. In this law it is not somebody else that makes you suffer; it is you yourself. Nobody can be cruel to you except yourself, and nobody can be kind to you except yourself. When you take this to heart, you will become acutely vigilant about not getting resentful or bitter or cruel, because you will know that no one will suffer from these things more than you.

Bringer of Tears

RUDRA

Another of the Thousand Names associated with karma is *Rudra,* which comes from the root *rud,* "to cry." We associate the Lord with love, so we find it difficult to understand how he can be called "he who makes us cry." But if God is all, he is suffering as well as joy. As Rudra, he personifies the unavoidable fact that most of us learn from our mistakes only because they bring us sorrow. Suffering is not the Lord inflicting punishment on us. Our ignorance in making choices is responsible for most of the sorrow we bring upon ourselves.

A certain amount of suffering in life is not only inescapable but even necessary for growth. It took me a long time to understand this, though my spiritual teacher tried to teach me very early in life. When I made a mistake and suffered for it, she would not be very sympathetic. She didn't gloat over my suffering or withdraw her support of me either; but in wordless ways, she helped me to learn not to make that mistake again. At the time I didn't understand what seemed a strange lack of sympathy. Today I know that if someone has been behaving selfishly, it is much better for that person to suffer the consequences and learn to change than it is to remain blind and fail to grow, which just means letting problems grow instead.

Every day I see the verification of the law of karma. Ill health is often an instance: if we do not take care of our body and maintain our peace of mind, our health is bound to suffer. That is Rudra making us cry. When our breathing is labored, when our digestion is upset, when our equanimity is destroyed, we do cry—and this crying is a signal, a red warning from body and mind, reminding us that something fundamental in our life is wrong. Pain, illness, insecurity, and mental turmoil are all loving signals from the Lord, who is telling us, "It's time you gave yourself a checkup. It is time you learned to change your ways."

Sometimes we manage to delay payment in the operation of karma, but then often it hits us with heavy interest. I prefer the idea of cash karma, where if you make a mistake, you pay for it immediately. However painful this may be for the moment, there is no interest hanging over your head. You give out six dollars worth of inconsiderateness, and on the spot you get six dollars worth in return. The debt is canceled. When you make a mistake, in other words, it is much better to take the consequences on the chin than to try to put them off, for consequences tend to compound, making the karma load bigger and bigger.

When I was growing up, it was considered imprudent in my village to have any kind of debt. No one would borrow unless they absolutely had to; the consequences of debt were just too serious. If you borrowed a small amount and paid it back quickly, the penalty wasn't bad. But there are certain moneylending practices in India whereby the interest on the loan ends up greater than the principal, so that the longer the loan is drawn out, the more you owe. You can borrow a thousand rupees, pay interest every month, and find out after three years that you owe not one thousand rupees but fifteen hundred. Similarly, in the spiritual realm, the weight of unpaid karma can be a tangible liability. When you accumulate karmic debts, therefore, pay them back right away, before the interest builds up. Don't be tempted to reschedule your karmic debt, and don't wait for interest rates to go down; it doesn't happen.

In India we have a peculiar phrase, "to file the yellow

paper." It means to declare insolvency, and it is looked upon—especially by creditors—as being less than fully honest. When you go to ask for a loan, the lender always asks you to declare that you have no intentions of filing the yellow paper.

One of the perennial paradoxes of the human condition is that if you want to avoid filing the yellow paper in life, the only way is to give. By giving you can never go bankrupt, because the more you give of yourself, the more you receive. In fact, it is only by giving that you can *avoid* going bankrupt. When you go through life refusing to give, the yellow paper comes and sticks to your forehead.

Most people who are insecure, for example, have difficulty giving of themselves. Insecurity is a warning from the bank within that you are getting low on funds. But such people needn't go on to the point that they become actually bankrupt in love. They can make themselves solvent again, even rich, by learning to give. As Saint Francis de Sales says, we learn to give by trying to give; we learn to give more by giving more. Instead of dwelling on ourselves and asking what we can expect from others, we should start looking for ways to give our time, energy, and resources to causes more important than ourselves.

Full

PURNA

The inner reality that we call the Self, who is the supreme Person behind every face, is always full. The Lord lacks nothing; he can never go bankrupt. You may remember Saint Teresa's beautiful prayer:

> *Nada te turbe,*
> *Nada te espante*
> *Todo se pasa,*
> *Dios no se mua*
> *La paciencia*
> *Todo lo alcanza.*
> *Quien a Dios tiene*
> *Nada le falta.*
> *Solo Dios basta.*

> Let nothing upset you;
> Let nothing frighten you.
> Everything is changing;
> God alone is changeless.
> Patience attains the goal.
> Who has God lacks nothing;
> God alone fills all his needs.

"Who has God lacks nothing." The Lord is ever full, and he gives freely of his fullness to all who love and seek him. But nothing he gives can diminish his infinite store of love and wisdom.

As long as we feel an emptiness inside, we cannot help living in insecurity; so we cannot help manipulating others in an attempt to fill that emptiness. Wherever there is manipulation, love cannot enter; in fact, when we try to use others to fill our own emptiness, even the little love we had is likely to vanish. To give freely we have to be full, and this kind of fullness comes ultimately from the Lord within.

Many years ago in India my wife and I had an experience which still reminds me of Teresa's phrase, "Who has God lacks nothing." We were spending a few days in Vrindavan, a sacred spot associated with Sri Krishna's childhood. In this sense there are two Krishnas: the eternal Lord, whom we realize in the depths of our own consciousness as our real Self, and a historical figure who was born about three thousand years ago in North India. Faithful Hindus believe that this historical Krishna grew up along the banks of the river Yamuna in an ancient town called Vrindavan, which today is full of beautiful temples and ashrams. Fortunately, this beautiful village has changed very little over the centuries, and it still attracts sincere pilgrims from all over India.

One evening my wife and I stayed on at one of these temples longer than we realized, and when we started for our host's home it was already quite dark. Night falls quickly in the tropics, and there were no street lights in that part of town. We made our way slowly down the crooked village lanes, and after half an hour or so of stumbling and groping, I decided that San Francisco's claim to have the crookedest street in the world is highly exaggerated.

Just when I was ready to confess that I really didn't know where we were going, a young monk appeared out of the shadows and announced that he had been sent by our anxious host to guide us home. He was a quiet man who evidently knew the streets well, and to show how glad we were to see him, I tried to engage him in the kind of spiritual shop talk that aspirants all over India exchange when they meet: where had he learned to meditate, what kind of disciplines did he practice, and so on. But he was so quiet that all my efforts at conversation failed. We walked home in the deep silence of this holy place, where almost no one lives who is not devoted to Krishna.

Our taciturn guide brought us to our door and was about to take his leave. I wanted to give him something to show our gratitude, but all we had with us was some milk sweets we had bought in the bazaar. I tried to place them in his hands, and then I discovered that this man I had thought so tongue-tied could express himself like a poet. "Brother," he said, "I live where Krishna lives. How can I lack anything?"

That young man's answer has been with me ever since. It is a small but eloquent reminder of how spiritual awareness makes us feel that we are always complete, that we need nothing.

Who Carries Us Across

TARA

Tara is "he who carries us across" the sea of birth and death. In the traditional invocation to the Bhagavad Gita, this image is invoked in a magnificent verse set against the background of the *Mahabharata*. The forces of darkness are compared to a fierce river; the five Pandava brothers, under the protection of Sri Krishna, are leaders of the forces of light. "In the river of battle," the poet says, "their opponents were great waves, crocodiles, treacherous whirlpools. But over this dread river the Pandavas crossed safely, with Krishna as their ferryman."

Just as there is a ferry line connecting Sausalito on one side of the Golden Gate with San Francisco on the other, Sri Krishna has a ferry going from insecurity to security, from hatred to love, from war to peace, from death to immortality. We are standing in the "river of battle" that is life, threatened on all sides by destructive passions, and Sri Krishna comes by with his little boat and says, "Hop in. I'll take you from this world of sorrow to the other shore of love and joy."

The Buddha too is represented as a boatman, always asking, "Anyone for the other shore?" The saints and mystics of every great religion can be thought of in this way. They pilot their boats not for themselves, but for the benefit of people like us who desperately desire to cross the river of life.

The Grandfather

PRAPITAMAHA

In my village, nobody referred to me as my mother's son; I was always "Granny's boy." My mother didn't sulk or feel slighted; she felt very proud. Nothing can take the place of a grandparent's experience.

When Dr. Spock was asked how he came to write about raising children, he confided that these were things formerly learned from grandparents; people turn to books now because grandparents are either cut off from their children or have interests of their own which they prefer to pursue. This is an incalculable loss. In my village we had a woman with seven daughters, each of whom had given her grandchildren. Whenever someone in the village had a complicated delivery or a sick child, it was not the doctor or the midwife who was sent for first. It was this grandmother, who had seen every problem under the sun.

With this name Sri Krishna says, "Just call me Grandpa, the grandfather of the cosmos. I brought into existence Brahma the Creator himself." In one of the most daring similes in Hindu mysticism, Brahma is actually called sexual prowess, the creative power which brings about this entire universe. Just as children are brought into existence by the creative power of sex on the physical level, the universe is said to have been born through the union of the divine Father and Mother—the union of Brahman, the formless Godhead, with Shakti, the Lord's creative energy.

This whole cosmos, then, is the offspring of the Lord. When I hear children quarreling in their sandbox, it reminds me of how physicists describe the first three minutes of creation, when all the elements and forms of energy we are familiar with today were born in the incomparable turmoil of the Big Bang. We can picture atoms screaming and colliding, universal forces fighting for their share of the turf, cosmic screams reverberating through the universe so loudly that astrophysicists can still pick out their faint echoes. If you think a few children in a sandbox can make noise, imagine what heavenly hullabaloo there must have been when the universe was being formed. Sri Krishna says, "Call me Grandpa, and treat me with great respect; for I brought all this into being."

Sacrifice

This name expresses a central principle of life. For orthodox Hindus the word *yajna* connotes the many rituals
that have been part of their religion for thousands of
years. These rituals, however, are only external symbols.
Their real meaning is the spirit of self-sacrifice. From the
earliest times, side by side with these rituals there has run
a mystical stream best summarized in the Upanishads,
which urges us to go beyond ritual and realize God in our
own heart through the practice of meditation. Rituals are
not of much help in the deeper stages of meditation,
where to realize God we have to go beyond all sensory
experience, beyond words, beyond emotions, and eventually even beyond thought.

In the Upanishads, those who perform rituals without
awareness of their deeper meaning are compared to "the
blind led by the blind." Ritual has a place in worship, but
according to the Upanishads it makes a most unsafe boat
for crossing the sea of life. There we need the tremendous
spiritual disciplines that have been handed down in every
great religion. This is an endless sea, where the dangers
are so great and the challenges so overpowering it takes
powerful disciplines like meditation and repetition of the
mantram to deepen our awareness, strengthen the will,
and clear our eyes so that they never waver from the goal.
All these disciplines are what is signified by *yajna*.

Yajna, then, is not just sacrifice but self-sacrifice.
Mahatma Gandhi, drawing on the Gita, made it clear that
yajna is not a ritual sacrifice performed in a temple, but

essentially selfless service in daily living: work for the welfare of others that is prompted not by a desire to make money or enhance our reputation, but by a desire to serve.

"Service" here means more than work which is just for our own family or a clique of friends. Equally important, it means working in harmony. Selfless, harmonious effort, the Gita says, contains within itself the seed and secret of success. However hard we work, however dedicated our attitude, it is not we who determine what we achieve; success is contained in the concept of yajna. "Give your best selfless effort in a selfless cause," Sri Krishna says; "then leave the rest to me."

I find ample illustrations of this in the history of our own meditation center, which we began twenty-five years ago in Berkeley. When I was leaving the University of Minnesota, where the Fulbright authorities had first posted me, I found myself packing my bags for California without anybody to look up there or any real idea of where to go. That day somebody gave me a copy of the autobiography of Yogananda Paramahamsa, who came to this country from India earlier in the century and founded a meditation center in California. Immediately I wrote a letter to the Self-Realization Fellowship in Los Angeles, telling them that I would be coming to California very soon. By return mail they sent a gracious letter inviting me to stay at their ashram. It was just like a little piece of India, where I could meditate without explanation or interruption and take long walks in a quiet, beautiful setting overlooking the Pacific.

Soon I was invited to deliver my first lecture in this country, in San Diego. I had expected one or two hundred people at most. About a thousand showed up, so many that I offered to speak again in the evening to accommodate those who could not be seated at the scheduled time. In those days, you know, more than twenty-five years ago, few Americans had been exposed to India's spiritual heritage; so I was immensely encouraged to draw such a large and enthusiastic audience.

After a few weeks in Southern California I came to the
University of California at Berkeley, where I felt right at
home: I have always been a campus man who enjoys
being around students, whether in India or in the United
States. But my academic duties at Berkeley were light,
and I was terribly eager to start teaching meditation.
Every morning I got up wondering, "Where are all these
earnest aspirants who must be wanting to learn to meditate?" I was sure they existed, but how was I to find
them?

Every morning in those days I used to enjoy a good,
long walk to campus. One day I was leaving the house as
usual when a bright red Thunderbird convertible pulled
up next to me. "Excuse me," a charming black lady said,
"but you seem to be new here."

"Yes," I said, "I'm from India."

She was intrigued, and soon I found myself talking
about meditation and the work I was so eager to begin.

"Well," she said, "what's keeping you?"

"I haven't got any place where I can teach," I said, "and
furthermore, I don't even have any students."

"My home is in Berkeley," she said immediately, "and
I'll give you all the facilities you need. I'd like to learn
what you have to teach, and I know some friends who I
think would like to learn too. Why don't you start this
Saturday evening?"

It happened so simply that I didn't have time to think. I
went to her home expecting a handful and found a room
full of good, eager people, both white and black—I was
proud to learn later that this was the first time any of
them had been in a gathering where blacks and whites
mingled socially. I began the talks with the Katha Upanishad, whose theme is nothing less than the conquest of
death. It's not a familiar scripture even in India, but the
following Saturday evening everybody had a copy of the
Upanishads, some heavily underlined; they had gone out
the day after my first talk and bought every copy in
Berkeley.

They were so enthusiastic that I introduced meditation

right away, half expecting them to excuse themselves and tiptoe out. But everybody stayed on, rising to the challenge of this most demanding of disciplines. Thus what would become the Blue Mountain Center of Meditation began: so naturally, so simply, just because my only desire was for others, to open the treasury of spiritual wisdom which the Upanishads and the Gita contain. We never asked for money. But little by little support began to come, friends began to offer their skills, and—most important for good work—dedicated people came, and stayed.

If we continue to work together harmoniously, I have no doubt that this work will be able to make an original, lasting contribution to the health and welfare of this country—and not only of this country, but through this country to the rest of the world. This is not something any one of us has achieved. It is the Lord who enables selfless work to prosper. If we do our best, the final responsibility is his.

And I think it has only begun. I hope with all my heart that our work will continue to grow, as more and more friends come to offer their time, talent, and resources without strings or reservations. It will be continued by our children and our friends' children, and those childrens' children; for this is how spiritual work grows and bears fruit from generation to generation.

The Auspicious

SHIVA

In Hindu mysticism, the sacrifice of self to a higher purpose is powerfully illustrated in the image of Shiva as Nataraja, the Lord of the Dance. There is a splendid statue of this image in the great temple at Chidambaram in South India. Shiva, his arms outstretched in a circle of fire, is dancing on the tiny, prostrate figure of a demon called Apasmara, "he who has forgotten." This pitiful creature is our self-will, the selfish, self-centered fragment of ourselves that has forgotten the unity of life. It is writhing in agony, but Shiva, the divine Self that is our real personality, is dancing in a transport of rapture.

Everyone, without exception, finds the reduction of self-will an extremely painful affair. But we can bear the pain if we remember that this demon of self-will is not who we are. As Shankara says in a famous hymn, "I am neither body nor mind nor senses nor intellect. I am pure consciousness and bliss; I am Shiva; I am Shiva!"

Self-will is the only barrier between us and God— that is, between us and security, between us and joy, between us and love. Those whose self-will has been inflated beyond the normal bounds find it extremely difficult to have loving relationships. As a result they find themselves isolated, and feeling isolated, they become hostile. Then they blame others for their hostility, which is really born of their own self-will.

This vicious cycle is the reason why the most effective of all sacrifices is the sacrifice of self-will. If you work every day at diminishing your self-will, you will find your relationships improving rapidly. Usually you will see benefits even in your physical health.

Very, very few people are naturally selfless. Virtually no one starts life with a perfect self-will score. But every one of us can improve our score with sincere effort. How many people work a little every day to get their golf score down! Reducing self-will to zero is the same idea— infinitely harder, but infinitely more rewarding too. And it doesn't require any special equipment. You can practice at home, at work, among friends, wherever you rub shoulders with others.

The family is an ideal setting for this kind of practice. At every turn you get the choice: Shall I put myself first, or shall I put my family first and myself last? It will be painful, but don't give up; go on trying. At the end of the week, take a deep breath and renew your resolution. That is what meditation is for—helping you carry on through next week, next month, next year.

Shiva personifies the power of the Lord to turn even the stiffest of trials to spiritual progress. He is called auspicious because meditation and the mantram can turn even pain, heartbreak, and bereavement into spiritual growth.

Destroyer of Evil

This name too evokes the Lord's austere aspect, typified by the awesome deity Shiva. Though Krishna is usually thought of as being more approachable than the fear-inspiring Shiva, he too will never let us forget that the spiritual life is often a battle, an inner struggle against all that threatens to undo spiritual growth.

No fight on earth is more arduous or demanding than this fight against self-will. When you are feeling battered, it can help immensely to remember that your second in this fight is Krishna. He is just behind you with his cut lemon and his towel and a little bottle of alcohol, and when you get thrown against the ropes he is there to revive and encourage you and push you into the ring again. "Don't lie there and go to sleep! Get back in there and fight."

You object, "I'm tired." All the more reason to fight! No words can convey how difficult this becomes in the latter half of the spiritual journey, when your meditation has taken you into the dark recesses of the unconscious and you can't make headway against the forces you encounter there. You try and try, but nothing you do seems able to take you to a state of deeper awareness. Every day you go on trying, and every evening you go to bed chastened but more determined than ever.

It seems impossible, but one day you are going to succeed. All those who keep on fighting against their self-will, who refuse to give up whatever happens, *will* win this battle some day. Then they will discover who has been their second, supporting them every step of the way. Here are Gandhi's inspiring words: "I have not the shadow of a doubt that any man or woman can achieve what I have, if he or she would make the same effort and cultivate the same hope and faith."

The Unconquered

APARAJITA

Here the imagery of sacrifice and of battle comes together. Only when the ego receives the final blow—traditionally thought of as delivered by Shiva—do we become invincible, *aparajita*.

The greatest sacrifice in life is the sacrifice of self-will. It is not too difficult to find people who are ready to give money or time and talent to a worthy cause, and there is merit in such sacrifices when they are offered without strings attached. But the offering the Lord really wants from us is our self-will.

This is not for his sake. The Lord is only thinking of our own well-being. As the Buddha says bluntly, for a self-willed person, suffering will increase like crabgrass. Self-willed people suffer everywhere. They go to the office and have trouble with the boss. They come out and have trouble with the meter reader. They go home and have trouble with their family; they go to the bowling alley and have trouble with the ball. When you reduce your self-will, you reduce your trouble—that is, you deepen your relationships, improve your health, and further your spiritual growth.

Some time ago there was a lot of excitement over the bout between Mohammed Ali and Leon Spinks. A few fellows coming to my talks, gentle chaps whom you would never suspect of having an interest in boxing, were following developments closely. I told them that compared to the fight that self-will puts up, external fights pale into insignificance. After fifteen rounds, you know, Mohammed Ali and Leon Spinks got to go soak in the tub, have their massage and a good dinner, and perhaps go out on the town. No matter how long, the fight is over. But in the spiritual life, after you have put in a hard day's work, had your evening meditation, and gone to bed, the fight is still on. You may be knocked against the ropes and throw in the towel, but this fight isn't going to end there. If you ask Sri Krishna when it will be over, he will answer, "When you have won."

In other words, none of us has any choice in this fight. Just by being alive, we are in the ring. In the Bhagavad Gita, Krishna shrugs and tells Arjuna, "This is the battle of life. If you say you won't fight, your own nature will push you into it. Your own karma will get you into situations where you can't help but fight." The struggle for self-mastery is not an optional duel, where you participate if you feel like it. It is absolutely obligatory.

Who Brings Sacrifice
to Fruition

YAJNA-VAHANA

In this name the Lord assumes responsibility for making
good work flourish, and for bringing about the spiritual
fulfillment of those who seek him in selfless service. Our
responsibility is simply to give our best.

As director of an important center of meditation, with
many serious aspirants under my guidance, I carry a responsible load every day. If I do not go around with
hunched shoulders, it is because I keep this promise of the
Lord's in mind and remember that the burden is on his
back, not mine. My responsibility is simply to keep myself out of his way and give him my all. I don't bear the
burden, no matter how much work I do. In fact, this
awareness allows me to do ten times as much fruitful
work as I used to be able to do in my old days as a college
professor—and I have always been a hard worker.

It is important to understand, however, that this
doesn't mean being irresponsible. We have the responsibility to do everything in our power to make things
right. We have the responsibility, in other words; it is the
burden that is the Lord's. When we have really done our
best, we can say with confidence, "I've done all I can.
Now I'm going on your word, Krishna. Protect me if
I've made a slip." My mother was fond of a song I used to
hear often: "I have thrown myself at your feet, Lord,
serving everybody around me; please guard me with
your love against all harm."

Good Works

Everything we do should be judged by how much it adds to the unity of life. If it conduces to unity, that work is spiritual. This applies to jobs, to recreation, to everything we spend our time on. When our motivation in eating good food and getting regular exercise is to strengthen the body for service, even these mundane acts become spiritual offerings.

On the other hand, brooding on oneself—cravings, resentments, greed, lust, anger, jealousy, and the like—can never produce good works. Not only that, this kind of self-indulgence drains the energy we might draw on for doing something beneficial. Like letting a car idle all night in the parking lot, brooding on ourselves burns up a lot of vital energy without our usually being aware of it.

When we can free ourselves from most of the personal preoccupations that are considered to be inescapable for a human being, immense vitality is released for selfless spiritual work. I like to call this getting a second engine, and it comes from the very depths of meditation. Twenty years from now, perhaps, you will be able to say something very astonishing to your family and friends: "I can do better work now than I could twenty years ago. I can work longer, more creatively, and much more effectively."

With progress in meditation, the second half of life can be much brighter and more joyful than the first, for the simple reason that you will be master of all your faculties. Your judgment will be sound, your willpower strong and resilient, and your relationships deep and lasting, founded on mutual respect.

The Place of Sacrifice

This name evokes another reference to ancient ritual. *Dharmayupa* originally meant the post where an animal was tied until the moment for sacrifice came. This tragic vestige of primitive religion still survives in a few isolated communities in India. Even in my village, in one of the temples there was animal sacrifice on some occasions when I was growing up.

Eternal credit goes to Mahatma Gandhi for putting an end to this. "If you really must follow these rituals to the last dot over the *i,*" he told us, "don't sacrifice one of God's living creatures; sacrifice a zucchini." We loved him so deeply that within a few decades, deft appeals like this had swept away undesirable practices thousands of years old.

Before Gandhiji's message reached my village, however, on certain days my grandmother used to send word to me in school to come home by a different route, in order to avoid the temple where this kind of sacrifice was offered. Once or twice I didn't receive the warning in time, and on the way home I saw the place where they had been sacrificing some poultry. It was a terrible sight. I couldn't understand how anyone could do such a thing to propitiate a loving God.

For me, the sacrificial post is the place where the ego is kept tethered, until we can finally sacrifice it at the altar of love. It sounds frightful because it *is* frightful. Reducing self-will is painful for everybody, but the alternative to

187

this pain is not only a different kind of pain later but increasing paralysis. When we cannot keep our ego on a very short leash, it has a cumulatively crippling effect on the will. And as the will grows weak, judgment goes, so that we begin to see things that are simply not there. This is the final tragedy of self-will. If you could only see into the minds of people with fierce self-will, you would see how distorted events look to them, how disfigured other people appear.

By comparison with this kind of blind and crippled consciousness, reducing self-will is well worth the cost. Setting aside the question of sacrifice, even keeping the ego tied to its post brings swift improvements in daily living. And as the idea of putting others first becomes natural, it is increasingly easy to relate to people and work with them even when they differ from us. Tethering self-will leaves us free to enjoy deep, satisfying personal relationships. What greater reward could we desire?

Freedom from Self-will

NIRVANA

Volumes have been written about this word *nirvana,* a simple word that literally means "blowing out" or "extinguishing." The image is of a fire that has gone out, the fire of the superficial, self-centered personality. Only when this small "I" is extinguished can we realize our true nature, which is divine. Only when we cease to identify ourselves with our separate personality can we realize the unity of all life.

Nirvana is usually considered a Buddhist concept, but the word also appears in the Hindu scriptures. In the Bhagavad Gita, Sri Krishna tells Arjuna, "When you constantly control your mind and senses through the practice of meditation and seek the Self within, you will attain nirvana, the state of abiding joy and peace in me."

It was the Compassionate Buddha, however, who took this image of blowing out a flame and made it into one of the most memorable metaphors in the annals of mysticism. Once, it is said, a young disciple full of philosophical questions kept asking the Buddha, "When one attains nirvana, where does that person go?" Generally the Buddha kept silent for such questions, but this time he took a little oil lamp by his side and asked his disciple to blow it out. The boy did as he was asked. Then the Buddha asked, "Where is the flame?"

"It is gone, Blessed One."

"Tell me where it has gone," the Buddha insisted. "Don't just say 'it is gone.'"

Freedom from Self-will

Until you attain it, discussions of what nirvana is don't have any application at all. When someone wanted to ask the Buddha about nirvana, he would say in effect, "I shall be happy to discuss it. Just extinguish all your selfish desires; then we can sit under the trees some evening and have a really learned discussion about what nirvana is."

The root *va* can mean "blow" also in the sense of the wind blowing. Imagine the mind to be as a lake, with a high wind constantly blowing over the surface, always keeping this lake choppy and turbulent. Our mind is just like a lake, over which the winds of selfish desire are blowing all the time. If it is not a desire for this, it is a desire for that. If it is not for one big desire, it is for two smaller desires. This fierce wind keeps blowing all the time, and the water of the lake is never at rest.

In the high regions of the Himalayas there is a lake called Manasarovar, "the lake of the mind," which is the goal of many pilgrims. Hindus of great faith bathe here before going on to the great temples of that region. The waters are icy, but such is their faith that they are able to enjoy this cold bath, which to people from the hot plains of India is very cold indeed. The surface of this lake is said to be always calm, beautifully reflecting the snowy peaks nearby.

This is the image of the mind in nirvana—calm, beautiful, holy. When the winds of self-will have ceased to blow and self-will has subsided, we can look at the bottom of the fathomless lake of consciousness and see for ourselves the supreme reality which is our real Self.

According to the Lankavatara Sutra, "Nirvana is where there is no birth, no death; it is seeing into the state of Suchness, absolutely transcending all the categories constructed by the mind; for it is the Buddha's inner consciousness."

Whose Thread
Is Good

SU–TANTU

Many names of the Lord begin with the simple syllable *su,* which means "good" in Sanskrit. He is good looking, his voice is good, his complexion is good, his thoughts are good; you get the idea. But a few of the names beginning with *su* are a little unexpected.

Sutantu, for example, literally means "he who has beautiful threads." The allusion is to a marvelous metaphor in the Upanishads, where the universe is compared to the web that a spider weaves out of itself.

After reading this image for the first time, I actually became interested in spiders. Their unobtrusive activities in hidden corners took on new meaning. I would watch a spider slowly bringing out one silvery, silken thread, then another, then another, until soon there would be a beautiful web. The Sanskrit word for spider, *urnanabhi,* literally means "the creature that brings wool out of its navel." The finest wool, you know, real Pendleton.

That is just what the Lord has done. On my way to the beach this afternoon, it filled my heart with joy to see so many black-faced wooly lambs frisking about on the hills. I didn't see them just as lambs; I saw the Lord, spinning out from himself millions of creatures as the "wool-spinner" draws out its web.

This morning when I was having breakfast, I looked out our kitchen window and saw that the grass outside was a filigree of silver where hundreds of new cobwebs glistening with dew caught the light of the rising sun. By afternoon they will be gone again. How fleeting life is! Everything in this delicate web of a universe changes from moment to moment.

Every Tuesday, on my way to my regular talks on meditation, I remind myself, "Another week is gone." This is not morbid reflection. It is good to remind ourselves how quickly life passes, for it throws our activities into the sharpest perspective. Every day's first priority is to learn to move closer to the Lord of Love who lives in the depths of our consciousness.

Who Keeps Expanding
His Web

TANTU-VARDHANA

Imagine if, through the miracles of genetic engineering, scientists are able to cross a spider with an octopus. Who knows? It's not impossible. They might be able to come up with a tremendous spider. In the Galapagos Islands, a friend once told me, he saw a turtle weighing several hundred pounds. A spider weighing that much might cover the state of California with its web. Extend this to include the cosmos and you get an idea of how Sri Krishna keeps on expanding his web that is our universe.

There is a ubiquitous billboard advertisement that just shows a picture and says "More." Sri Krishna would say, "That's my motto!" If we ask, "More of what, Lord?" he would reply, "Just *more*. More people, more lambs, more sheep, more elephants, more trees, more bees, more stars, more space and time. . . ." That is the theory of the expanding universe. Sri Krishna's web expands and expands for forty or fifty billion years; then it starts contracting again, until everything goes back into the spider and the spider too disappears. Everything comes, then everything goes—except the Lord in his impersonal aspect, waiting to begin the cycle of creation all over again.

Destroyer of Sin

A few days ago a friend wrote to me that she had found a typographical error in the first volume of my *Bhagavad Gita for Daily Living,* published many years ago. Our lives too have "typos," mistakes we have committed—perhaps long ago—whose marks remain today. Every day that passes is a precious opportunity to correct these typos, by drawing on meditation for the will and the inspiration to change our lives. Whenever we do this, as this name implies, the power for change comes from the Lord.

Resentment, as Jesus reminds us, is a very serious typo. The longer it goes uncorrected, the more glaring it becomes. And self-will is a real printer's devil. In this sense, the beautiful Prayer of Saint Francis is a proofreader's manual for finding and correcting errors. I recommend it to everyone—Christians, non-Christians, even atheists—for meditation because it spells out perfectly how to undo the conditioning of selfishness to which all of us have been subjected:

> Lord, make me an instrument of thy peace.
> Where there is hatred, let me sow love;
> Where there is injury, pardon;
> Where there is doubt, faith;
> Where there is despair, hope;
> Where there is darkness, light;
> Where there is sadness, joy.

O divine Master, grant that I may not so much seek
To be consoled as to console,
To be understood as to understand,
To be loved as to love:
For it is in giving that we receive;
It is in pardoning that we are pardoned;
It is in dying to self that we are born to eternal life.

Correcting habits like impatience, unkindness, lack of sympathy, or preoccupation with our own personal pursuits does not require a cataclysmic reformation. It is in little matters that we show impatience or unkindness, and it is in the correction of these little mistakes, as of an "i" not dotted, that spiritual improvement lies. Remember those wise words quoted by Benjamin Franklin: "For want of a nail the shoe was lost; for want of a shoe the horse was lost; for want of a horse the rider was lost." Ben Franklin was a keen observer. He must have seen this borne out often, in everyday matters as well as in the affairs of state.

Immortal

AMRITA

I can understand why children and teenagers find it difficult to grasp the transience of life. They live as if things would always be the same and tomorrow would never come. After you have lived through thirty or forty years of life, however, you begin to notice how many people you once knew have passed on. Almost regularly now I get a letter saying that another of my former classmates or my childhood friends is gone.

Most of us do not want to notice this, but after the first volume of our life is closed, it is necessary to notice and reflect, and then to make changes to focus the remainder of our lives. "Time," says Marcus Aurelius, "is a sort of river of passing events, and strong is its current. No sooner is a thing brought to sight than it is swept by and another takes its place, and this too will be swept away." And he adds, almost in the language of the Buddha: "The universe is change; our life is what our thoughts make it."

We cannot put our trust in any changing relationship between bodies, or even in a relationship based on sympathy of mind or intellect. All these shift continuously. The only relationship that is permanent is the relationship between the Self in you and the same Self in others—the spiritual relationship in which we forget ourselves in living for the welfare of all.

In discovering that relationship, we enter immortality here on earth. The body, which is physical, *will* die; nothing can alter that. But the Self is not physical; it cannot die. When we *know* ourselves to be that Self, know it in the very depths of consciousness awake and asleep, then there is no break in awareness when the body is shed at death. Dying is no more than passing from one room to another.

Here is the song of Kabir on overcoming death:

> O friend, hope for Him whilst you live;
> Know whilst you live; for in life deliverance abides.
> If your bonds be not broken whilst living,
> What hope of deliverance in death?
> It is but an empty dream that the soul shall have
> Union with Him because it has parted from the body.
> If He is found now, He is found then;
> If not, we do but go to dwell in the City of Death.

Free from Craving

VIRATA

Epictetus has an excellent metaphor for teaching detachment, perhaps the most important skill to acquire for living in a world of change. "Remember," he says,

> to behave in life as you would behave at a banquet. When something is being passed around, as it comes to you, stretch out your hand and take a portion of it gently. When it passes on, do not try to hold on to it; when it has not yet come to you, do not reach out for it with your desire but wait until it presents itself. So act toward children, toward spouse, toward office, toward wealth.

Epictetus would have been at home at a Hindu banquet, for we have three unwritten rules.

One is that there is a regular apportionment of space on the piece of banana leaf that serves as a plate. You don't pile things on top of each other. Each delicacy is served in a particular order in its appropriate place.

Second, when something delicious is put in front of you, you don't start in gobbling immediately; you wait until everybody has been served. Children get so impatient that a mother sometimes has to train her little one by slapping his wrist gently; but by the age of five or so all are able to sit patiently waiting until the serving is done and everyone observes a few moments' repetition of the mantram. After that, as Sri Ramakrishna says, conversation stops; the only sounds you hear are of eating and drinking.

The third rule is that when you are done, you have to wait until the last person has finished the last bite before you get up. This unwritten code of banana-plate manners makes even the largest family feast go smoothly.

In personal relationships, Epictetus suggests, we should observe the same kind of restraint. Don't try to cling to people, to hold people to you: everything changes, and if you try to arrest relationships and hold on to others, making them conform to your own needs, you will lose all the magic of life. William Blake says it beautifully:

> He who binds to himself a joy
> Does the winged life destroy;
> But he who kisses the joy as it flies
> Lives in eternity's sunrise.

The Supreme Magician

Many years ago I took some friends to an excellent magic show. We had seats in the middle of the theater, but young Josh went and stood right near the stage to be able to expose the magician. Not only did he not succeed, but the magician managed to impress Josh even more than the rest of us.

He began by bringing ordinary little creatures out of his top hat—rabbits, hamsters, doves, the usual contents of a magician's hat. Josh was about to yawn when the animals suddenly became bigger and more offbeat: owls, vultures, a couple of overfed poodles. By the time he brought out a full-grown horse, everybody was sitting up and taking proper notice. He threw a large red blanket over the horse, and when he whipped it away the animal was gone. There was consternation all over Josh's face.

That is what the Lord's magic is like. In Sanskrit, the passing show of life—the illusion that we are all separate creatures rather than an indivisible divine whole—is called *maya,* with which our word "magic" may be connected. Out of apparent nothingness the Lord brings you and me and all these innumerable other creatures out upon the stage. Then, all too soon, he sweeps us away. Those with whom we have grown up, gone to school, shared the joys and trials of our adult years, one by one they just go.

It was this vision of the transience of life that burst like a bomb in the Buddha's consciousness. He saw in his imagination his beautiful wife lying dead, he saw his young son walking into death's jaws, and then and there he turned his back on everything else to seek a path that all can follow to discover that we are not the perishable body but pure spirit, the immortal Self.

When the Lord throws the blanket of maya over us, once he lifts it again we are gone—but only so long as we identify ourselves with the body. We don't have to disappear. If we can learn to identify ourselves with the Atman, the Self, then when the blanket is removed we will still be one with the magician himself, the Lord. In the climax of meditation called *samadhi,* when the mind becomes still and self-will is extinguished, we discover that our real Self is the Lord of Love.

Life is so short, and this discovery so urgent and so difficult, that none of us can afford to waste a day in not doing our best to move closer to the goal. Please take advantage of every opportunity to repeat the mantram, to train your senses, to keep on transforming your passions. And please be regular about your meditation. Don't lose a single day; don't waste a moment doing selfish things. All this time can be utilized for discovering the Self and for going beyond death here on this earth.

Whose Work
Is Complete

The Lord is simply "the one who has done his job." If we love him and give him our best effort, it is the Lord within who enables us to do the job that every human being has come into life to do: to become aware of him. When that is done, the Upanishads say, everything has been done. "When you have known the Self, everything in life is known," because it is this Self that is the essence of all things. To realize the Self is to love all creatures—in fact, to become love itself.

How are we to make this supreme discovery? Saint Thomas Aquinas tells us in a famous passage,

> Three things are necessary for salvation: one, to know what we ought to believe; two, to know what we ought to desire; and three, to know what we ought to do.

The scriptures and mystics of all religions concur on what to believe: that the core of our personality is divine, and that the purpose of life is to discover this divinity for ourselves. What to desire, then, is the Lord himself, which is why mastery of desire has been called the key to Self-realization. Meditation enables us to withdraw our desires from frustrating, foolish channels and redirect them toward the Lord in an overwhelming, overriding flood of longing to be united with him forever.

When this is understood, the third requirement—what we ought to do in life—becomes clear. The implication is unavoidable: until we discover the Self, no matter how successful we may have been by ordinary standards, we have failed in our main job. Making money, collecting pleasures, visiting exotic places, making a name for ourselves—these are not our real job. They only leave us hungrier than we were before, more alienated, more lonely; for deep in our heart is the awareness that anything less than Self-realization will leave the human being unfulfilled.

Lovable

Krishna is an exceptionally attractive and affectionate Person; but to take it a little farther, those who realize their oneness with Krishna, the Self, become lovable too. We naturally want to be with such people; we find it natural to fall in love with them.

"Once you realize the Self," the Upanishads say, "you will never be lonely again." Loneliness is epidemic today; even people with bundles of money and lofty social status get stricken by this virus. Once we realize the Self we don't have to beg, "Josie, please love me. Bernard, please be my friend." When the lotus blooms, Sri Ramakrishna reminds us, it has no need to say "Bees, come to me"; they are already looking for blossoms. Similarly, when you discover the Self you will find that you draw people to you naturally for inspiration, consolation, and strength.

By the same token, we can move closer to the Lord by moving closer to other people. This is not always easy, especially at those times when we feel inclined to hole up inside ourselves. It *is* sometimes difficult, even exasperating, to work with others with different methods and ideas. As we learn to give and take and to pay more attention to the needs of others, however, security comes without our seeking it; we no longer feel isolated in a meaningless world.

These developments reflect a divine paradox: all of us live in the Lord, just as he lives in each of us. The intellect gets baffled by this kind of contradictory language. In the Bhagavad Gita, when Krishna tries to explain, Arjuna raises his eyebrows and looks blank. Sri Krishna tells him gently, "This is the mystery of my being. You cannot understand." No amount of reasoning can make it clearer, but when we test it in our lives, we understand. The proof is that when we live harmoniously with others, it is we who grow spiritually. We do help them, but it is we who move closer to the Lord in our own lives. When we avoid opportunities to work and live with others, we lose this precious opportunity for growth, which can come to us in no other way.

Whose Mind Is Full
of Wealth

The Lord's wealth is his limitless love, the only kind of wealth that grows with the passage of time. It is not subject to fluctuations, like currency or stocks and bonds. The Lord presides over an endless bull market of love.

Saint Augustine gives us practical advice on how to become really wealthy by learning to love God through cultivating these qualities:

> Temperance is love surrendering itself wholly to Him who is its object; courage is love bearing all things gladly for the sake of Him who is its object; justice is love serving only Him who is its object, and therefore rightly seeking; prudence is love making wise distinctions between what hinders and what helps itself.

He Who Attracts

KRISHNA

Of all the Thousand Names, the name *Krishna* has come to be etched most deeply on my consciousness. This is due to the blessing of having grown up at my teacher's feet—as I would say, through her grace. I cannot take credit for my devotion to Krishna; she must have planted it in my consciousness early in my childhood.

When you go on repeating the mantram sincerely and systematically, this is the kind of devotion that the Lord helps to generate in your heart. Once it floods your mind completely, it will not leave you even in your sleep; it walks with you and works with you always. In the Hindu tradition we call this *ajapa-japam,* the name of the Lord repeating itself.

One special instruction I would like to give to you is to make use of every spare moment to repeat your mantram. A million opportunities can be discovered during the course of a single day.

One of the biggest opportunities, of course, is at night, when you are falling asleep. There may come a time when you cannot sleep and find it almost impossible to go on repeating the Holy Name hour after hour; the mind gets tired. At such times, what I used to do is ask Sri Krishna in my heart to make it a joy for me to recite his name. As a result, when I repeat his name today it is not a discipline; I do it with all the joy of indiscipline. I have no limits now, no restraints, no sense of when to do it and when not to do it. I do it all the time, which is what going beyond all disciplines means. But you have to struggle with disciplines for a long, long time before this kind of spiritual freedom comes.

Since we are talking about Krishna, let me treat you to one or two of the stories with which virtually every Hindu child grows up. In one great scene from the *Bhagavatam,* which contains the story of Sri Krishna's life, Krishna the teenager goes to the city of Mathura, where a cruel king called Kamsa is bringing untold misery to his people. Kamsa sends a fierce wrestler named Chanura to give the boy a special welcome. Chanura is the heavyweight champion of the ancient world. He just stands there waiting for Krishna, eager to make a pretzel of him; and the people of Mathura, who have heard that the youngster is invincible, gather to see what will happen.

In Indian drama Chanura is usually played by a fellow about six feet four and weighing two hundred and fifty pounds. The stage shakes as he moves. He plants himself in front of Krishna, blocking his path, and in front of these thousands of Krishna's admirers he roars: "I hear you have tamed the serpent Kaliya and conquered every demon sent your way. I would like to see how you fare with me!"

The onlookers tremble for Krishna at this challenge, because the boy is slender and svelte. He has a wasp's waist and perfectly proportioned arms and chest; every part of him is just right. He looks so boyish, so fresh, so tender-hearted. "And look at King Kong over there!" the crowd cries. "His *arms* are the size of Krishna's whole body!"

Krishna steps into the ring, and it is one of the highlights of the *Bhagavatam* when, after the preliminaries are over, he picks up Chanura as if he were a little mouse. I will spare you the details, since I am sure you have witnessed this sort of confrontation on TV. Briefly said, Krishna makes short work of him, and the wicked Kamsa realizes that his days are numbered.

When we love the Lord with all our heart, every scripture promises, this is the strength he gives us—not of body, but of will. Nothing will be able to break us; we will be able to stand up to any challenge and hold our own.

Sri Krishna's mother, it is said, was so devoted to her son that when Krishna was learning to walk, she used to wrap her arms around him so his beautiful body would not be bruised. "What a miracle, Krishna!" exclaims a great mystic poet of Mysore in a song. "You who protect the entire universe, your mother thinks that by falling once you are going to get hurt."

In other relationships, too, Krishna was mischievous about hiding his strength in tenderness. He had an older cousin, Bhima, who is a great favorite with Indian audiences. Bhima is huge and muscular, highly physically oriented and often forgetful of his strength and size. He is always doing exercises of some sort: if he isn't running he is swimming; if he isn't swimming he is wrestling or practicing with his mace. He is simple, direct, and very loyal, and he has an awful temper. He is also slightly older than Krishna, and according to ancient Hindu custom one should always show respect to one's elders, greeting them by touching their feet. Still, when Krishna shows this kind of reverence to Bhima, it seems a little wrong. *Everyone* touches Sri Krishna's feet, even kings and sages.

"Krishna," someone finally asks, "you are the lord of the whole universe. Why do you touch the feet of this big cousin of yours?"

Sri Krishna replies, "If I don't duck he embraces me, and I get a few broken ribs!"

The word *Krishna* comes from the root *krish*, "to attract." Krishna is he who draws love from everyone, who draws us to him in the hearts of others. Strangely, when we try to draw love out of others, we get into a tug-of-war that may end in pushing them away, for all we are doing is trying to meet our own needs. It is forgetting ourselves in the needs of others that draws their love irresistibly. Again, this is the paradox of maya: try to grab and you will lose; give, and you will hold others' love forever.

Truth

God is love, Gandhi used to point out penetratingly, but He is also truth: *satya* means not only "truth" but also "that which is real." One of the oldest prayers in Hinduism says, "Lead me from the unreal to the real": from a lower state of consciousness in which we are acting out our dreams, to the state of truth and joy.

Most of us are convinced that we are already awake, that we are completely responsible for our thoughts. But we don't seem to be able to have the same thought for a very long time. If a beneficial thought comes, we can't make it stay, and many, many thoughts sneak into the mind that we do not approve of at all. Therefore, the Buddha would say, it isn't quite correct to say that we think thoughts; it is more accurate to say that thoughts think us. To be able to say "I think" and mean it, we should be able to have a regular roll call of thoughts and account for every one of them.

Imagine the mind as a kind of theater. When I go to the art museum theater, the attendant checks tickets not once but twice. After the first show she comes around again, and if you don't have your ticket stubs she will ask you, politely but firmly, to leave. We should have the same capacity to check on our thoughts. If an unkind thought is lurking in a dark corner, we should be able to shine our flashlight on it and say, "No ticket? Sorry, you'll have to go."

When a mood or desire overpowers us, we think it is one thought, one state of mind that can't be altered until it has run its course. A dominant passion or obsession seems a solid block in the edifice of our personality. The Buddha would say no. Every mental state is a momentary flash of thought, one after the other, and no two thought-moments are connected. Think of a million separate thoughts, he would say, standing in line to get into the theater of the mind.

In a movie theater, when the projector is running, you see a smooth, continuous flow of action: horses galloping, people jumping on their horses and falling off again, guns firing, stagecoaches being robbed. But stop the projector and you will see that the film is only a slide show. The action seems real merely because the separate frames are moving by so fast. Similarly, in a person whose mind is fast, thought after thought pushes through the turnstile so rapidly that we think it is one solid wave of emotion over which we have no control. Once the first thought pushes through, the rest follow in a heap.

Get hold of the first fellow, the Buddha says. He hasn't got a ticket—in fact, he has a permanent season no-ticket, a very Zen phrase.

In yoga psychology this thought-leader is called a root *samskara,* the source of a whole chain of compulsive thought. Even after you have learned to keep lesser freeloaders out of the mind, a root samskara is terribly difficult to deal with. If you succeed in locating him and demand to see his ticket, he will answer, "Who do you think you are? Let *me* see *your* ticket." And everybody seated around him will explain, "Oh, he's been here a long time. He must belong; how else could he have gotten in?"

In other words, the roots of compulsive thinking— anger, fear, lust, and the like—go deep in the unconscious. To deal with them with authority, you have to reach an even deeper level of consciousness in meditation. If you can get below a samskara, you can be there waiting for him and say, "Sam, where is your ticket?" He will look sheepish and say, "You got me!" Once you can do this, you know with joy that every trait due to negative conditioning can be undone.

Approachable

ASAMMITA

Most of us know how difficult it can be to approach a person in authority. Mussolini, I think, designed a virtual palace for himself, where anybody wanting to see him had to walk down a long, long hall at the end of which Il Duce sat, looking down from a raised throne. By the time frightened supplicants reached this awesome figure, their bones would have turned to water.

The British government in India used similar architectural tricks to intimidate us: long ascents of stone steps to the viceroy's palace, for example, just a little too high and a little too deep to be taken in a stride, while armed guards with splendid uniforms watched from unapproachable heights. Even Gandhi often found it impossible to get an audience with the viceroy of India, and the rest of us felt we were doing well to get a few minutes with a local British official—in our own country.

Gandhi, by contrast—probably the greatest man this century has produced—made himself accessible even to children, and shed every vestige of authority that might set him apart from others. In those days the British Raj was at the zenith of its power, and all its medieval pomp and pageantry was brought out on state occasions to impress millions of its subjects. Gandhi appeared before us in his simple white dhoti and nothing else.

Sri Krishna too, lord of the very universe, encourages us to turn to him whatever our past or present is like. We have only to turn our face and heart to him and he will respond. In India we say that when we take one step toward the Lord, he takes seven steps toward us. But he will watch to see whether we keep on taking steps—and that first step is left to us.

The Shining One

Deva, literally "a shining being," is usually translated as "god," and *devi,* the feminine form, as "goddess." Many, many devas and devis are mentioned in the Hindu scriptures, but as one of the oldest of these scriptures, the Rig Veda, says, "Truth is one, though the wise call it by many names." All these deities are simply names for the powers of life, which are expressions of the power of one supreme Lord.

In India it is perfect manners to add the word *Devi* after any woman's name. The significance is that every woman is an embodiment of the Divine Mother. This is a subtle way of reminding us men to treat all women with invariable respect. Never to use harsh language, never to quarrel, never to exploit, never to manipulate: this is the ideal at which all of us should aim.

In my village, when I was a boy, a woman could go out at any time without fear of being molested or even stared at. This reflects a high image of womanhood, that women should not be treated as sex objects, not as inferior or superior, but always with love and respect. If a society preserves this ideal, women live up to it naturally, and the whole culture benefits by their contribution.

Today, it seems, we are playing a kind of game, trying to show respect for women by changing certain offensive words. Bureaucrats talk a good deal about acceptable replacements for words like "serviceman" and "repairman." But it is not a change of words that is required; it is a change of heart. No special term coined by linguists can conceal a condescending mind.

I sympathize with everyone who has problems with the opposite sex; our modern civilization has made these relationships increasingly difficult. But I find it hard to sympathize with those who do not try every day to solve these problems by respecting the opposite sex and learning the art of nonviolent opposition when they find themselves in a situation that needs to be changed. Domination and competition injure both sexes. Man should not dominate woman, nor should woman dominate man; each should help to complete the other. This is the spiritual ideal.

Full of Glory

BHAGAVAN

Bhagavan is used much the way we use "Lord" in English, generally in reference to a divine incarnation like Sri Krishna or Sri Rama. In the tradition in which my grandmother and I stand, no one refers to a human being as Bhagavan, only to a divine incarnation.

According to one ancient text, the word *bhagavan* should be used only in referring to those who possess six *bhaga*s or "splendors." These are the prerequisites for any divine incarnation, and they are rather demanding.

The first is wealth—not in the worldly sense, but in the sense that an incarnation of the Lord has the capacity to give limitlessly. We can see this illustrated abundantly in the lives of Jesus the Christ and the Compassionate Buddha. Our usual idea is that those who aggressively acquire things for themselves, usually at the expense of others, are to be considered rich. In the spiritual sense, however, these same people may be paupers.

The second quality is power. In modern parlance this means physical power—power to dominate, to threaten, to destroy. But this kind of power is short-lived. Spiritual power—the power to help, to serve, to love—outlives any physical power, because it supports life. Love of power can be seen in many human beings, but a divine incarnation is marked by the power of love.

The third quality is dharma, the unity of life. Hatred, violence, unkindness, disloyalty, greed—any act or urge which sets us apart from others in pursuit of our own self-aggrandizement—all violate the central law of existence, that all of us are part of an indivisible whole. Those who are always aware of dharma will do nothing to violate this unity, no matter what the provocation. It is one of the loftiest tests of spiritual awareness.

Fourth comes esteem: not the superficial fame of the celebrity, but profound and lasting respect. A divine incarnation may not be recognized as such by many, but the scriptures say that he will be widely respected for his wisdom and compassion. In the *Mahabharata,* India's ancient epic about the war between the forces of light and the forces of darkness, Sri Krishna is depicted as commanding the respect of both sides, though he makes it clear which cause is just.

The fifth quality may be surprising: beauty. The Lord is infinitely beautiful, with a beauty that is not diminished by time. Physical beauty cloys with familiarity, but the inner beauty which shows itself in the capacity to give and to cherish grows with the passage of time. It transcends the senses, transcends even mind and intellect.

The last quality is absolutely essential. *Jnana* is sometimes translated as knowledge, but its real meaning is not intellectual learning but wisdom in living—a rather rare quality. A divine incarnation must be a complete master of the art of living, which means that he or she must possess continuous awareness of the unity of life and the detachment required to live in harmony with that unity, without any thought of personal gain.

These are the six qualities that must be present for one to be called Bhagavan. They are marks of perfection, and since no human being is likely to be perfect, I think you will see my grandmother's wisdom in never applying the term to anyone but Sri Rama or Sri Krishna.

On the other hand, there is practical significance in these six *bhagas*: these are qualities we should try to cultivate in our own lives if we want to remake ourselves in a higher image. To give rather than grab, to help rather than hinder, to be aware of the unity of life, to depend for our beauty on the qualities of goodness and kindness, to put ourselves last and the whole around us first—this is how we develop these divine qualities which are the natural endowments of Bhagavan, the Lord within.

Destroyer of
Good Fortune

BHAGA-HA

Paradoxically, there is another Holy Name derived from *bhaga: Bhagaha,* "he who destroys good fortune." In the ancient Vedas, the goddess of good fortune—later worshipped as Sri Krishna's divine consort, his feminine aspect—was called Bhaga; people prayed to her for health, wealth, beauty, and fame. Why then should Krishna, the all-loving Lord, have this terrible name, as if he bestows worldly blessings with one hand and then tears them away with the other?

The answer is that in the Hindu and Buddhist view, we are here on earth for one supreme purpose: to realize the unity of life. And by some quirk of human nature, the vast majority of us begin to think seriously about life only when things are going against us.

My grandmother tried to teach me this painful truth at an early age, and I resisted for many, many years. "No, Granny," I would say, "that can't be true." It didn't faze her. "One day," she said, "you are going to agree with me."

Today, after many years of bitter experience, I say to myself almost every day, "Yes, Granny, you were right. This is the best way in which we human beings can be educated." It would be wonderful if we could learn from good fortune, but generally it is only when fortune is snatched away that we begin to reflect, to question what we are doing and ask if it is taking us where we really want to go.

Sit back for a moment and reflect with some detach-ment. It is painful to realize that whatever growth we may have achieved personally came not when the wind was in our favor, not when we were in the best of health, not when our partner used to leave little notes saying "I love you" around the house. It came rather when we were hit by ill health, or deserted by our friends, or estranged from our family, or cast down by the shatter-ing of great hopes. During these agonizing moments we seem to be able to grow, particularly if we want to grow and are eager to learn.

We can look upon the Lord as that force which makes us think for ourselves and learn from our mistakes. It is the same Lord within who enables us to change direction and find health, happiness, love, and wisdom.

Bringer of Joy

ANANDI

This name is sure to be met with appreciation. Everyone wants joy. Yet despite Madison Avenue, which promises it from cars, clothes, drinks, drugs, and even soaps, joy is something rare. It is not just elation or euphoria, but an exalted state beyond pleasure and pain in which the mind is still.

If this sounds drab, that is only because we haven't tasted it. When the mind is still, there is no selfish craving to be or have or enjoy something that we lack. We are at peace, lacking nothing, full of love and the desire to give. When we reach that state in meditation where we can deal successfully with our personal hang-ups and harness some of our strong urges for pleasure and self-aggrandizement, we will begin to taste the indescribable joy that is our legacy as human beings.

In the Krishna tradition there is a passionate devotional poem called *Gita Govinda,* "The Song of Krishna," in which every symbol of lovemaking is used to convey the joy that comes when the separate personality loses itself in the divine. Jayadeva, the great Bengali poet, is trying to convey his devotion through symbolism that can be understood by ordinary human beings like us, who find that the keenest physical pleasure they can enjoy is sex.

Mystics do not deny that sex is an intensely pleasurable experience. The question they ask is simply, "How long does it last?" So keen, so enjoyable, and yet so brief—just a few moments of sensation. Our desire is for joy that never ends. Only when our desires have been unified, when all our fierce longings have been welded together, can we attain the state of lasting joy which is called *ananda*.

Child of the Infinite

To understand this name, we have to do some exploring in Hindu mythology.

In ancient India there once lived a loving couple named Aditi and Kashyapa, so devoted to the Lord that when Vishnu chose to be born on earth as Vamana, one of his many incarnations, he chose Aditi and Kashyapa to be his parents.

At that time the earth was oppressed by a king named Mahabali, and the Lord's descent into human life was to put an end to his reign of terror. Later, when it came time to destroy the tyranny of Mahabali, the tiny Vamana would be transformed to cosmic proportions. But at birth he seemed just like any other infant, weighing seven or eight pounds and skilled in keeping his parents awake with his cries at night.

As he grew, too, just like any other boy, he kept getting into trouble—all of which only added to the joy of Aditi and Kashyapa. They were such devoted parents that the little boy, to show his adoration, once asked, "Mom, what gift can I give you?"

Aditi said, "You'd better not ask that, Vam. I wouldn't really like to tell you."

But Vamana continued to ask, and finally he did something no incarnation should ever do: he slipped up and said, "I promise I grant whatever you wish."

"In that case," Aditi replied, "the next time you are born, I want to be your mother then too."

So, eons later, when Vishnu has to come to earth again to reestablish righteousness, he again is born as Aditi's son. But this time Aditi is the princess Devaki, and Vishnu is born as Krishna.

To me, all this seems only reasonable. Wouldn't the Lord want to be born into a familiar home? He knows from past experience that everything there will be just right. He can't afford to take chances with a new mother; the forces of evil threaten him from the moment of birth.

Even for ordinary people like us, it seems logical that a loving relationship in this life might carry over into the next. In my village, where reincarnation is taken for granted, most people believe that if you try to be a good mother or father, you make it possible to pick up that relationship the next time around. My mother would say that there must have been a perfect relationship between me and my spiritual teacher in former lives, for I was literally born into her arms. I could come into that context through her grace only because I had been with her before.

Aditi comes from *a-*, "no," and *diti,* "limit." Aditi is the Divine Mother, and the practical significance of her name is that we should not restrict our love to just one or two people; we should learn to love without limit.

God is the mother of all. We too should look on all children as our own, and share responsibility for them. We are teaching the next generation by our personal example; so we have to ask ourselves constantly, "What effect will my actions have on the children around me?"

Pele, the great Brazilian soccer star, can name his price to any advertiser, but he turns down all offers to endorse cigarettes or alcohol. When asked why, he responded simply, "I love kids." He knows that millions of children around the world, without exaggeration, look up to him and will follow his example.

Good Fortune

LAKSHMI

One part of the Lord's being is masculine, called Vishnu. But the Lord also has a feminine aspect, and that is called Lakshmi, personified as Vishnu's eternal consort. These are not really two but one.

Lakshmi is the goddess of good fortune and beauty. When the gods churned the cosmic ocean at the beginning of time to distill the nectar of immortality, she arose like Venus from the waters of life and chose Vishnu to be her eternal companion. Her symbol is the lotus, the most beautiful of all flowers; and this lotus is the womb of Vishnu, from which the cosmos is born. When Vishnu comes to earth as Krishna, Lakshmi is born as Rukmini; when he is Rama, she is Sita.

Enduring

Sahishnu is a beautiful name that reminds us how compassionate the Lord is, for it comes from the root *sah,* "to be patient, to put up with, to endure." Sahishnu is the Lord who bears with us and forgives us our mistakes.

This name encourages us too to be patient and bear up cheerfully when life hands us something that we would rather not have to deal with. To judge by our responses to life's ordinary ups and downs, most of us say, "Give me only things I like. Don't give me anything I dislike; give it to Brian instead."

Even good people, when they have been struck down by illness or misfortune, sometimes ask, "Why did this happen to *me?*" This is a most peculiar question. What we should ask is, "Why should this happen to anybody?" Simply asking this question at a deeper level of awareness brings the patience to bear tragedies without self-pity, releasing the insight and compassion to help others and to grow ourselves.

Pleasant and unpleasant together are the very texture of life. Only when we give our best whatever comes, good or bad, can we live in freedom.

Who Brings Good
from Suffering

Su means good; *tapas* is suffering freely borne for the sake
of others and one's own spiritual growth.

When you attain Self-realization and look back upon
your life, you will find it most satisfying to see how even
your mistakes have played a part. If you hadn't dipped
your fingers in hot water when you were eight, so to
speak, you would have soaked yourself in much hotter
water later on. The purpose of mistakes is to learn not to
go on making them. Eventually we *know*—as Gandhi
says, "from bitter personal experience"—that pain and
pleasure, disappointment and satisfaction, success and
failure, cannot be isolated from each other, and that chas-
ing after worldly satisfactions can never bring fulfillment.

Most of us look upon pleasure and pain as two different
departments at war with each other. They are really one
department, with only one chairperson, and any attempt
to isolate what is pleasant and avoid what is unpleasant is
doomed to failure.

For this reason, I never ask those who meditate with
me if they are having fun. The only relevant question is,
"Are you growing?" It is this forced fragmentization—
"Let there be one department for what I like, which I
must have, and another department for what I don't like;
let it go to others"—which makes us into pygmies. To
grow to our full height, we have to learn to bear what we
dislike cheerfully. If it benefits others, we can actually

learn to enjoy it. Then a good deal that was bitter in life becomes sweet.

Whose Thoughts Are True

SATYA-MEDHA

While we are on this subject of pleasure and pain, let us consider for a moment the dream world. The Hindu scriptures say that when we dream, various experiences may come; we may go through travails of sorrow or scale the pinnacles of joy. This is characteristic of everyone's dreams. And as far as the nervous system is concerned, many dream experiences are not much different from their waking counterparts. The sensations and physiological responses are the same. I have heard children laughing or crying in their sleep; I have heard older people talking in their dreams. At that time, those sorrows and joys are real.

When we wake up, however, the dream world melts away. We cannot really say it was unreal: after all, we did experience it. The sorrow or happiness were as real as anything in ordinary life. But when we wake up, these feelings evaporate. The dream experiences seem shadowy and distant, and we see that in reality there was no cause for sorrow or pleasure at all.

Similarly, the scriptures continue, when we attain Self-realization, we shall look upon the experiences of our past life, its pleasures and pains, its successes and defeats, exactly as we look upon a dream. When I look back on my early career, in which I made the same kind of silly mistakes and suffered the same kind of blows that everyone makes and suffers in life, I do not feel any regret or pain. It's all a dream. I don't have any animosity against those who hurt me, because I would feel absurd resenting someone from a dream. That is how you will come to look at your previous life: you wake up, and all the burden of the past falls away. It will free you from so much turmoil, release so much energy and vitality, that you will feel you have a new lease on life.

This is true not only of dreaming but of daydreaming. Do you remember Thurber's famous story, "The Secret Life of Walter Mitty"? Everybody has a secret life, you know. We may not always be aware of it in all its details, but most of us have at least our innocent fantasies. Some of my students in India used to get carried away building castles in the air; one of them liked to take a piece of paper, write his name, and then add "MA, PhD, LLD, Oxford, Cambridge." It was an innocent attempt to add weight to an otherwise airy academic career.

I have also known somebody in this country who had a very poor voice, but who, when no one was around, used to go out under a tree and sing as if she were Joan Baez. She would play her guitar and sing exactly in that style. I had to sympathize. Think of the frustrated hopes, the secret dream of standing in the Greek Theatre and singing "We Shall Overcome" while the audience stands teary-eyed and cheers . . .

Dreams and daydreams, of course, are often a kind of escape, an ingenious attempt by one part of the mind to try to compensate for what is lacking in the other part—that is, for the disappointments of everyday life. Dreaming is a safety valve for the frustration that otherwise can rage when certain dear hopes and deep desires are not fulfilled. I find this a very compassionate explanation. In this sense, dreams and daydreams do have a useful role to play when there is no higher outlet for the energy dammed up in a thwarted desire.

My advice, however, is to forget your dreams—don't dwell on them—and never dwell on daydreams or fantasies of what might be. When you do, you are teaching your mind to live in a dream world, where it can cling to private pleasures and retreat from anything unpleasant.

Most Walter Mittys have trouble with work and relationships; when a little pebble in the real world blocks
their path, they give up and turn to fantasies.

In Indian folklore, the danger of daydreaming is illustrated in the story of a dairy maid who is going to the
market to sell her milk, carrying the pot on her head. She
is young and beautiful and fond of dancing, and since she
isn't repeating her mantram, her mind begins to wander.
"When I have sold all of my milk," she thinks, "I shall
have two rupees. After a month, if everything goes well,
I shall have sixty rupees. Sixty rupees! What could I do
with sixty rupees? . . . I could buy a real silk dancing
costume; perhaps I would even have enough left over to
buy dancing bells for my feet. Then this is how I would
dance . . ." She begins to skip, the pot falls from her head
and shatters, and instead of sixty rupees she has none for
buying a new pot.

Reality

Sat means absolute reality: literally, "that which is." The word comes from the root *as*, "to be," which is related to the English verb *is*. One of the most accurate statements we can make about God is simply *God is*.

God alone is real. Shankara defines the real as that which is changeless. Anything that changes, if not precisely unreal, belongs to a lower level of reality.

If we apply this demanding definition to the universe, we have to admit that the earth and sun and even the Milky Way galaxy will pass away some day. As an amateur astronomer, I find it fascinating to reflect on change and reality at this cosmic level. Imagine: a galaxy that is a billion light years away from us can be photographed at an observatory, but that photograph will not be a photograph of the galaxy as it is today; it shows the galaxy as it was a billion years ago. When I see spectacular photographs in books on astronomy, I remind myself that these are photographs of the past. They are, in Shankara's view, photographs of something that is unreal, because it has changed before we could even see it.

If you want to know what reality is, what the universe and you and I are really like, you must look for something changeless. The only real part of us is the part that does not change. The more we can identify with this changeless core of personality, the more "real" we become.

Most of us, I suppose, have known at least one friend on whom we could depend always. We feel they are reliable, and we trust them to stand by us through thick and thin. In a sense, this is recognizing an element of the changeless in such a person.

On the other hand, we know how difficult it is to have relationships with people who vacillate. We never know where they stand. Their personality seems uncertain, unfounded. If we can learn to keep our mind even, to keep our love and loyalty as steady as possible, to that extent we are moving closer to the reality within us—the core of Sat, the supreme reality that is God.

Even if people offend us and we don't feel like being warm toward them, it is in our interest as well as theirs to be as steadfast and loyal as possible. This steadiness of mind will help us to discover the nature of life as it really is.

Sat also means good. That which is good is real; that which is real is good. Gandhi pointed out this connection. Evil, he said, has no reality of its own; it exists only insofar as we support it. If we withdraw our support, evil cannot continue.

This little word *sat* points to a great truth taught in the Hindu scriptures—that you and I are, at our core, good. Our truest nature is good. We have only to remove the covering layers that are hiding this innate goodness. We should think of our original goodness and not dwell on original sin: for the goodness is our real nature; the sin is a temporary stain.

Unreality

ASAT

In a daring moment, the Hindu mystics also call the Lord by an opposite name: *asat*, that which is unreal. This is a paradox that can cause theologians sleepless nights, but I like to look upon it in a purely practical way. In a sense, we all do live in an unreal world, a world that is colored to such an extent by our individual mental conditioning as to become unreal. But it is only when we wake up to a higher level of consciousness that we can realize this. Until then, we must continue to act as if our experiences are real.

It is helpful to remember, however, that just as the experiences of the dreamer and daydreamer are not real, but only constructions imposed by the mind, so the pleasures and pain of this world have no reality apart from the mind. This world is made up of neither pleasure nor pain. These are contributions of our own nervous system, and they depend very much on personal conditioning.

When you reach a certain depth in meditation, you will look back upon some of the occasions when you felt a great deal of pain and see it as a kind of optical illusion. You will not see any reason for the pain, which means that there was no pain in the world outside. You did suffer then, just as in a bad dream; but now that you are awake at that level of consciousness, you can look on the same experience without any overlay of suffering.

In the same way—and even more revolutionary—when you look back on the occasions when you enjoyed a great deal of pleasure, you will wonder why you looked upon it as pleasure. It was only excitement, the nervous system stirred up in a particular way. What you will prize then is not excitement but joy, which wells up when the mind is not agitated by desire or aversion, but lies still.

This is why, in the Gita, Sri Krishna tells Arjuna to bear not only pain but pleasure with an even mind. When you are enjoying something, he says, don't get excited. Put up with it patiently; it will soon be over. We want to object, "That's taking all the joy out of life!" It is just the opposite. We can enjoy, but we should not cling. If we cling to the sensations of excitement, we are teaching the mind to cling to the sensations of pain, which are bound to follow as night follows day.

Pleasure and pain, the Gita says, have nothing to do with us. They are affairs of the body and senses, something that happens when the senses come in contact with objects of sense-perception. The Self, the inner observer, is not involved. When the senses come in contact with objects they enjoy, it is only natural to identify ourselves with the body and senses and attribute that joy to ourselves. But the same is true in pain. When our ego is hurt, it suffers, and the more we identify with the ego, the more *we* suffer. Only when self-will is low, when we gain detachment from the ego's demands, does sorrow begin to leave our lives once and for all.

This doesn't mean that we become callous or unfeeling. I live in a world without pleasure and pain but full of joy. I grieve greatly at the tragedies I see around me; in fact, I grieve much more today than I ever used to, because I am a million times more sensitive to the suffering of those around me. But even in that sensitivity there is joy, because it releases limitless resources that enable me to help. Our globe faces terrible problems, but with the dedicated assistance of many friends who support this work, I know today that we *can* make a difference in helping to solve them.

The Supreme Path

Gati, from the root *gam,* "to go," means both "path" and "destination": it is where we are going and that by which we travel. The Lord is the way and the goal.

After attaining Self-realization, great mystics have exclaimed: It was you, Lord, who roused me to seek you. You were my running and the path on which I ran. You were there with your starting gun forcing me to get started. I didn't have my socks on, let alone my running shoes; in fact, I wasn't even out of bed, but you roused me and wouldn't let me sleep in peace. You laid the track; and when it began to get too hard, you laid down soft grass; but when I got used to comfortable turf, began taking it for granted, you spread stones. When my endurance was coming to an end, you gave me a second wind. You arranged the whole race, and in the last quarter you gave me the superhuman strength I needed to throw myself forward and breast the tape. You held the starting gun and it was you holding the tape at the end. I thought it was I who won the prize, but now I realize that everything was done by you.

Joy

RAMA

The scriptures say that Vishnu has come down to this earth several times to reestablish dharma, righteousness, in times of great evil. These ten incarnations or *avatara*s happen to follow the pattern of biological evolution. They are the fish, the tortoise, the boar, the man-lion, Vamana, Parashurama, Rama, and Krishna. The ninth incarnation is said to be the Buddha, and the tenth, yet to come, the scriptures call Kalki.

Rama—the name comes from the root *ram,* "to rejoice"—shares with Krishna the distinction of being the best-loved incarnation of Lord Vishnu. He was born a prince in ancient times in the city of Ayodhya in North India, and his story is known throughout South Asia in the *Ramayana* epic.

Rama is a lovely word in Sanskrit and perhaps the most universal of mantrams. It is repeated alone (Mahatma Gandhi's mantram was *Rama, Rama, Rama*) or with the name Krishna added, as in the mantram my grandmother gave to me:

> *Hare Rama, Hare Rama,*
> *Rama Rama, Hare Hare,*
> *Hare Krishna, Hare Krishna,*
> *Krishna Krishna, Hare Hare.*

Rama is the perfect mantram, because it means the joy that knows no end. Pleasure is something that comes and goes. Joy stays with you, increasing with the passage of time.

You may remember my saying earlier that in yoga psychology, the human personality is said to consist of five jackets or sheaths of consciousness. The outermost jacket is the physical body, the sphere of pleasure and pain; the innermost jacket is very rarified consciousness, described as made out of joy. That is the jacket everyone wants. When you go to Macy's, that is what you are looking for among the designer labels. Everyone asks, "Have you got the jacket of joy?" But the sales clerks have never heard of it.

The great mystics tell us that we don't have to go to a store to buy this jacket; we already have it. But our closet is so full of garments of nylon and polyester that we don't see it. Only when we remove the synthetic clutter of our internal wardrobe do we cry out in ecstasy, "Here it is! Right in my closet all the time."

After this discovery, we live in perpetual joy. This is not a figure of speech. This joy can never leave us—as the Buddha said, it will follow us like a shadow, even into our sleep.

We don't have to leave our family, quit school, leave our job, or go off to a mountain cave to find this joy. We can find it right in the midst of life. The Upanishads actually calculate that the joy of Self-realization is a million times greater than any happiness we have known before. To their authority I can add the testimony of my own small personal experience.

Bearer of the Bow

DHANUR-DHARA

This name is an epithet of Sri Rama, who is usually shown in sculpture and painting carrying his bow because he is a great archer. His arrows, *Ramabana,* are the mantram. This is a perfect image, because archery and meditation both require keen concentration. In meditation what we are trying to do is bring all our attention together to focus on one single point, the Self. When we love the Lord with all our heart, all our mind, and all our strength, we are consummate archers, victorious on the battlefields of life.

In Hindu mythology it is Rama, not Krishna, who is known as a great warrior, leading his army to victory against the evil king Ravana. Krishna, the gentle cowherd boy, is not usually thought of as a fighter, and although there are many stories of him slaying demons, his overall image is of a peaceable, loving incarnation. Even when his beloved Arjuna faces the apocalyptic battle that is the climax of the *Mahabharata,* Krishna does not take part in the fight but serves as Arjuna's charioteer.

Yet there are times, the poets tell us, when Sri Krishna recalls his former warrior life. Unlike the rest of us, he has free access to the deeper levels of the unconscious, and sometimes scenes from his past lives bubble up to the surface.

In a beautiful poem, the blind mystic Surdas, who lived in medieval India, captures Krishna in such a moment. Yashoda, Krishna's foster mother, is trying to put baby Krishna to sleep, and the poem is a haunting lullaby that describes the scene. Krishna doesn't feel sleepy, so Yashoda begins to lull him with the story of Rama, which is told in Hindu households all over India. She starts just as every other mother starts: "Once upon a time there was a king named Dasharatha who had four sons, and the oldest was called Rama . . ."

Krishna's eyes start to close; he is drifting off into the never-never land between waking and dreams. Yashoda tucks him in and begins to tiptoe away. *"Waaaaah!"* Krishna wakes up. Yashoda rushes back, soothes him, and continues, swinging his cradle as she speaks: "Rama had to go to the forest with his beloved wife, Sita, and his brother Lakshmana . . ." Krishna's eyes are closing; he is adrift between worlds again. "But in the forest, while Rama and Lakshmana are away, the demon king Ravana comes and carries Sita off in his chariot, and she cries for help with all her heart: 'Rama! *Rama!*' . . ."

And suddenly baby Krishna sits up wide awake, his eyes full of fire. "My bow!" he cries. "Lakshmana, bring me my bow!" He is no longer Krishna; he is back in his previous life.

Self-control

DAMA

Most of us acknowledge the virtue of self-control, but to judge by our actions, what we would really like to control is others. If we could just succeed in making those around us do what we want, where is the need to master ourselves?

This is what anger is all about. If Jack gets angry with Alice, what he is saying is: "You're not doing what I want, and I'm going to make you!" If Alice responds in kind, she is saying the same thing. To mediate their quarrel, all I have to say is: "Jack, why don't you try to control yourself? Alice, why don't you work to control *yourself?*" It's that simple.

Not only is it simple, nothing else is very realistic. The only person whose thinking I can control is myself. You can regulate someone else's watch, but you can't regulate anyone's mind except your own. Even that takes a lot of hard work, but if you find your mind getting speeded up—say, in anger—it *is* possible to slow it down to a reasonable pace, and maybe one day even to stop it completely. When you can do that, you will know what joy really means.

Whom We Desire

ISHTA

In my native language, Malayalam, *ishta* also means "friend." So Ishta is a very good name for the Lord. He is a good friend, and the contribution a good friend can make is twofold. A friend should support us in time of trouble, but a real friend will also oppose us when we are causing trouble or about to cause trouble, whether to others or to ourselves.

My grandmother was a perfect friend. On the one hand she was very softhearted, but on the other hand I have never seen anybody so tough in all my life. In fact, the two toughest people I have ever known are Granny and Gandhiji. She didn't spare her toughness when she was dealing with me, either. She was usually very tender, but sometimes she was strict to the point of seeming harsh. It took many years to understand that this was an important part of her love for me.

In the scriptures, however, *Ishta* means your chosen spiritual ideal, the incarnation of God to whom you feel most deeply drawn. In India the question "Who is your Ishta?" doesn't mean who is your friend, but who is your favorite incarnation. It might be the Buddha, or Shiva, or Krishna, or the Divine Mother, or Jesus, or Rama, or quite a number of other divine manifestations. The main thing is that the Ishta is the goal of our spiritual desires.

The Sufis say that we should see the Beloved in everyone we love. In all our relationships, though we are aware of the inadequacies at the present, we should never lose sight of the fact that the Beloved is hidden in the hearts of all. This is what enables us to keep faith with people, to trust and support them, and to oppose them tenderly when necessary to keep them from making a serious mistake.

King of Death

Yama means literally "the controller," and in Hindu mythology, Yama is the god of death. This is such a fearsome name that in most Hindu homes it is never mentioned. You must have read those Victorian novels where the father says, "I don't want to ever hear his name in this house again," and after that everyone is careful not to mention Uncle Cecil by name. Similarly, people in my village would never talk about Yama directly; they would just say "he" or "it."

But the Lord, out of his deep love for us, will not let us deny the truth of death. He may strike us hard, if necessary, to make us aware that time is our executioner.

My grandmother was a great spiritual teacher, for she planted this awareness in me very early in life. I never forget how quickly time passes. We grow up, go to school, grow old, and life is over before we know it, perhaps before we have begun to understand why we are here. And we sit here without a struggle, when all our energy should be bent to discover how to go beyond death here in this life.

Krishna comes as Yama to remind us that as long as we identify ourselves with the body, we cannot escape death. Far from being morbid, this reminder is a great gift. It is one of life's greatest blessings to be constantly aware of death, so long as we use that awareness to deepen our meditation and make every day count in our contribution to life.

245

No gift, the Buddha says, is greater than the gift of helping someone to understand the nature of our existence. Particularly with our children, it is not in giving things that we show love so much as in showing them, through our own dedicated example, that life's highest goal is to break through our identification with the body and discover our identity with the deathless Self.

Every day in my meditation I remember my teacher with all my love and devotion, because it is she who gave me this gift and enabled me to share it with all who are prepared to give their energy and enthusiasm to Self-realization. Every morning when she returned from the Shiva temple she would come to me, put a flower from the morning's worship behind my ear, and bless me with words that still reverberate in my heart: "May you be like Markandeya." Markandeya is a great sage in the Hindu scriptures, who attained immortality at the age of sixteen because of his profound devotion to the Lord.

Freedom

The *Thousand Names* is composed in verse form, with a great deal of poetic play of sounds that makes its recitation in Sanskrit very beautiful. In one verse the poet plays with two names from the same root which echo each other in sound and seem opposite in sense. The root is *yam*, "to control." Yama, the previous name, means "controller"; *aniyama* means "free from control," "without constraints"—not lacking in discipline (*yama*), but being free from circumstances.

No one appreciates being dictated to by circumstances, pushed about according to stimulus and response. But it took me a long time to understand that to be free from this kind of conditioning requires great self-discipline. Today, however, I never ask the question, "What will tomorrow bring?" I don't mind if conditions are unfavorable or if people are being unkind. Whatever comes, I know I can give my best.

Aniyama means being without expectations, which is a very positive state. It means you can see things clearly and act intelligently for the benefit of all, without ever being at life's mercy.

Kindness

AKRURA

Here we have the secret of the spiritual life in just one word. The great medieval mystic Johan Ruysbroeck, when asked how to become perfect, gave the same answer: "Be kind, be kind, be kind." When we remove all unkindness from our deeds, words, thoughts, and feelings, what remains is our natural state of love.

This may sound simple, but it demands many years of sustained effort to eliminate all unkindness from our inner and outer lives. Some would say that this is humanly impossible—that it is beyond human nature to return kindness for unkindness even in our thoughts. Only when we see someone who has attained these heights do we begin to say, "Maybe it is possible, after all." When we come in contact with such a person, we know there is no limit to the human capacity to love.

This is the role of the spiritual teacher, and it carries great responsibility. A spiritual teacher cannot ever afford to give in to anger or impatience. Whatever the provocation, he or she must maintain this never-changing attitude of love and forgiveness. The word *guru* literally means "heavy"—one so heavy that no storm can uproot him, as heavy as a mountain that withstands the hurricane without flinching.

Strength is often equated with the capacity to attack, but to me it means the internal toughness to take whatever life deals out without losing your humanity. It is those who never stoop to retaliation, never demand an eye for an eye, who are truly strong. They have the toughness to be tender, even sweet, while resisting violence with all their heart. By contrast, those who are ready to strike back at the slightest provocation are not strong but fragile. They may espouse a higher view of human nature, but almost anything can break them and make them lash back at those they oppose.

When someone is being sarcastic or cruel to you, the natural response is to retaliate. If you want to be unshakable, you have to train your mind in patience and endurance, the most grueling training that life offers. Life shows no mercy to those who lack this inner strength. Every virtue requires the toughness never to retreat in the face of challenge.

It is a very poor evaluation of human beings to think that impatience and violent reactions are part of human nature. We have to look to people like Mahatma Gandhi, kind under any provocation, to see what human nature is really like. Gandhi's life showed over and over that even a violent person will respond if exposed to someone who, by being always kind, focuses consistently on the highest in our nature.

As meditation deepens and the mantram begins to get established, some interesting developments take place in the mind. Resentments and hostilities that used to torment us will be getting weaker; yet they will still be present. It is a peculiar position. You find a little resentment, a little sympathy—a curious mix.

For example, suppose somebody is rude to you. You don't like the fellow, but you don't dislike him either—a great advance from your previous attitude. You may feel hostile for a moment, but you know that hostility no longer has the power to push you into doing or saying something you will regret. And because you know you are in control, that experience will leave no residue of resentment in your mind. I don't mean you will like that person, not at first— in fact, for five minutes or so you may positively dislike him. But afterward you say to yourself, "Oh, the fellow comes from a broken home, went to a rough school, fell in with the wrong company; that's why he has become like that."

Once you know you can transform negative feelings in this way, you have won a great victory. Even so, you can't expect to sail through the world in complete tranquility. When people criticize you unfairly, you are not expected to say "Thank you." When they denounce you, you're not expected to praise them. Such responses would be unnatural and unrealistic. The spiritual life requires artistry, and often we may have to answer personal attacks with tender but firm opposition. We should never connive at discourtesy or unkindness, for others' sake as well as for our own.

This kind of opposition requires detachment, toughness, and real love. But when these are present, they generally disarm the other person. In time they may even win him over as a friend, which to me is one of the greatest thrills life offers.

The name *Akrura* has devotional overtones for every Hindu. In the *Bhagavatam,* Akrura is famous as a charioteer who served the historic Krishna with single-hearted love, regarding him not as an ordinary mortal but as an incarnation of Vishnu himself. For Vishnu to be called Akrura, then, is a little like Christ being called Francis or Teresa—a beautiful reminder that, as Krishna says in the Gita, "Those who love me with all their heart, they live in me, and I in them."

Many of the best-known stories in India are about the life of Sri Krishna, and they invariably cast a spell of delight and wonder, of mystery and humor. One favorite of mine deals with Akrura when Krishna was still a young man, leading the pastoral life of a cowherd in the little town of Vrindavan. When the time came for him to assume the role for which he was born, Akrura, because he had some awareness of Sri Krishna's real nature, was chosen to drive his chariot to Vrindavan and bring the Lord back with him to assume the throne of Mathura.

The road to Mathura was hot and dusty, and while they were traveling, Akrura became thirsty. After a while they saw a temple near the side of the road. Akrura went inside to look for water, leaving Sri Krishna in the chariot.

Within the temple courtyard was a pond. Akrura knelt down to drink, but there in the water he saw Sri Krishna. Confused, he rushed out to the chariot again. Sure enough, Krishna was still there, waiting patiently in the chariot.

Thinking he must have made some mistake, Akrura went back again for a drink. But there again he saw Krishna, smiling out at him from the water.

Like a bewildered child, Akrura runs back and forth a few more times, unable to believe his eyes. Finally, in all the innocence of his love, he goes to the chariot and asks, "Lord, how is it that you are here and in the water at the same time?"

Sri Krishna, with a twinkle in his eyes, says, "Look around, Akrura." Akrura looks and there is Krishna in the trees, in the sun overhead, in the birds singing, in the very air. Everywhere he looks, there is the shining face and sparkling eyes of the Lord.

Invincible

AJITA

This is a popular name for boys in India. Every budding sports star likes to be called Ajit, because it means "he who can never be beaten." Unfortunately, however, some of the Ajits I knew in college never made it to the playing field.

To spiritual aspirants, *ajita* stands for the strength of those whose will cannot be broken. One of the magnificent secrets Gandhi gave us is that strength does not come from bone and muscle; "it comes from an indomitable will." This is not the will to get one's own way whatever the cost; that is what mystics call self-will. When self-will is extinguished, what remains is a will that nothing can break—which means that nothing can vanquish you. I remember a famous Oxford scholar, Professor Gilbert Murray, warning the British government to beware of Gandhi because he could not be tempted by personal pleasure, prestige, or power. Such a person can never be bested, because his will can never be broken.

Resolute

DRIDHA

We all know how long first-of-the-year resolutions usually last. That is because our resolve simply does not go deep enough. We mean what we say, but our subconscious mind objects, "I am not a party to this. That vow is a purely intellectual decision, arrived at without consulting me. Don't count on me for support."

In deep meditation, however, you can get your subconscious to sign on the dotted line. Then your resolution becomes unbreakable: what you say, what you think, and how you feel are one. It is said of Mahatma Gandhi that what he thinks, what he does, what he lives, is all the same; so his will could not be broken even by the greatest empire the world has seen.

Irresolute

ADHRITA

But if the Lord is resolution, he is also just the opposite: Adhrita, "he who is irresolute too." This is his compassion. On the one hand there is the law of karma, which says that if I have led a life of selfish indulgence for many years, it is going to affect my body and my mind and my relationships. This law doesn't spare anybody; the Lord is resolute about his laws. Yet when we learn to love him with all our heart, he becomes irresolute and says, "All right, for you the law of karma no longer applies." Then we are released from the ill effects of past mistakes—but only so long as what we do in the future is guided entirely by love.

The Lawgiver

In the Rig Veda, oldest of the Hindu scriptures, Varuna is the embodiment of purity and order in every sphere of life, from the laws governing the physical universe to the moral order and the laws of righteousness governing the mind and human affairs.

Varuna is also a name for the setting sun. Just as the setting sun seems to collect the rays of light and withdraw them back into itself, Sri Krishna withdraws the entire universe of name and form into himself at the end of one cycle of creation. Similarly, when the mind is completely still in meditation, the universe of name and form, cause and effect, disappears, and our personal karma is dissolved.

Krishna is also called "the son of Varuna," which is not only figurative but has a specific reference to Hindu mythology. Varuna, it is said, had two fascinating sons: Vasishtha and Agastya. Vasishtha was a great sage who became Sri Rama's spiritual teacher. His answers to Sri Rama's questions, illustrated with many stories, comprise one of India's classic manuals of spiritual instruction, the *Yoga-Vasishtha*.

Agastya, the other son, was a precocious sage and a rather colorful figure. He was very short, but nothing daunted him; he was always ready for anything. Once, it is said, he drank the ocean dry. To this day, whenever a very short person in India tries to be aggressive, someone is likely to object, "Who do you think you are, Agastya?"

The Tree of Life

VRIKSHA

Trees are vital for the life of this whole planet. It is not just that they purify the atmosphere, taking in carbon dioxide and giving back oxygen. Today it is clear that the world's great forests have life-supporting effects many thousands of miles away.

When rain forests in South America are razed, for example, by large-scale corporate operations, the monsoons in southern Asia are affected, pouring their rain into the Indian Ocean instead of on croplands along India's east coast. The precipitous destruction of the world's forests may also contribute to the "greenhouse effect": carbon dioxide and other pollutant gases in the atmosphere, by trapping the sun's radiant energy, may be raising the temperature of the earth, threatening consequences like chronic drought in the wheat belt of the Midwest.

Finally, the massive clear-cutting of rain forests destroys whole species of life, with unknown effects on the biological diversity of the planet. Rain forests, as reported in a conference sponsored by the National Academy of Sciences and the Smithsonian Institution, make up only 7 percent of the earth's land surface, yet they are home to more than half the earth's species. According to the prominent biologist Edward O. Wilson, about 40 percent of the rain forests are already destroyed, "and an area about the size of West Virginia is cleared each year."

At stake, among many other things, are perhaps twenty thousand food plants the world may well need to supplement the mere twenty species on which most human beings depend. Other losses might include the desertification of the tropics and crop failures due to a lack of insect pollinators. It simply is impossible to predict what might result from an "extinction crisis" that Professor Wilson believes "poses a threat to civilization second only to nuclear war."

While scientists are spelling out the details, we might reconsider the practicality of an age-old view, held until a few centuries ago in cultures around the world: that the whole of nature is a life-supporting system worthy not just of respect but of worship. This is not primitive thinking, and it is quite compatible with scientific progress—at least, within a framework that takes into consideration the whole planet and its future. The earth *is* our mother. Its incredible diversity nourishes all creatures, including the human species. It is in our own interests to shape our uses of technology around the welfare of all life.

In biology, interdependence—which Gandhi always stressed in human institutions—is not just an ideal. It is a fact of life, a fact of love. Trees are an illustration that any child can understand. They give us oxygen, fuel, and the restorative solitude of great forests, which attract water and wildlife to replenish barren places; it seems natural to me to find them holy.

In a hot climate like India's, when you have been walking out under the blazing sun, it is a welcome relief to stretch yourself out under the benign branches of a mango or banyan tree. This perfect symbol of refuge and refreshment was caught in English in this version of a haunting Muslim prayer:

> May God be your shade from tree to tree,
> May God be your guide from well to well.
> God grant that beneath the desert stars
> You hear the Prophet's camel bell.

Vriksha also refers to a powerful image from the Upanishads, the Tree of Life, which "has its roots above," in the Infinite, "and its branches here below." This tree is called *ashvattha,* an interesting word for linguists to quarrel over. In the spiritual derivation, it means "that which will not be standing tomorrow." The whole nature of life is given in just one word: "Everything passes; God alone never changes."

There is a story about a mystic who never stayed in one place, but kept wandering all his days. He had an acute way of reminding the rest of us about the transience of life. When he got old, people began to ask him, "Holy one, you are getting on in years. Why don't you settle down? We'll build you a little house and take care of all your needs."

"I already have a little house," the sage objected, pointing to his body. "Why should I build another one just for twenty or thirty more years?"

All

I remember a billboard that promised, "You are somebody at everybody's bank." The Lord is everybody in
everybody's bank. It is not at all easy to keep in mind, but
everyone around us, everyone we meet, is sanctified by
the presence of the Lord in the depths of the heart—
whether they are aware of it or not, whether they act like
it or not.

"Practicing the presence of God," as Brother Lawrence
so aptly phrased it, means learning to behave with understanding and patience *all* the time. It is worth repeating
that this does not rule out a dash of loving, nonviolent
resistance. I remember how sharply my grandmother
would chastise me when I did something that was not in
anyone's best interests. At that young age I used to retort,
"My friends don't talk to me that way!" Out would come
her pointed answer: "I am your friend; that's why I talk to
you that way. If they don't, then they are not real
friends."

When a person is riding roughshod over others' needs,
most of us find it unpleasant to call him on his behavior.
We know it will upset him, and that he in turn will do his
best to upset us and others; so we take the path of least
resistance. "It's a free country," we say; "he can do as he
likes." I have heard this argument countless times. "If he
is determined to throw himself in the pit, let him fall." It
was only after I began to meditate that I really got the
point of my teacher's words: if we say we care about

other people, we have to care enough to tell them when they are doing something that will bring sorrow to themselves and others.

After I finished my university education, I had the opportunity to meet important figures from many parts of the world. I had admired them through their books and speeches and through their work in many spheres of life—writers, artists, scholars, educators, scientists, and diplomats who for one reason or another had impressed me with what they had done. Yet when I met them, I often couldn't help feeling let down. With my university degrees, it surprised me to see that they knew so little about living compared to my Granny, who didn't know how to read or write. Gradually I began to understand that perhaps it was she, rather than those the world lionized, who was the best source of living wisdom for me. I began to meditate, and only then did the points that she had never tired of making to me as a child, which I had never quite grasped, really come home.

With this one word *Sarva,* the scriptures remind us that every person on the face of the earth is entitled to the resources of nature. Every person is entitled to the support of nations which are more advanced, because the Lord lives in all. It is because we do not realize this that we industrialized nations consume the lion's share of the world's resources—for example, an estimated eighty percent of its energy. When we begin to act as if the Lord lives in all, we shall find that there are enough resources on earth to satisfy everyone's needs—including the opportunity for work that needs doing and for the reasonable leisure that all human beings deserve.

Until Gandhi came, I don't think Westerners were even aware that we in Asia and Africa and South America too need access to natural resources for leading a comfortable life. Before then, with few exceptions, even intelligent, well-intentioned observers in the colonial powers took it for granted that we in the rest of the world needed little in the way of resources because we didn't know the right thing to do with them, which was to extract them from the earth and turn them into items that could make money. Obviously it would have been wasteful to let us sit on resources that we weren't going to use, especially since others knew what to do with them. It was almost a moral obligation for the industrialized powers to take what God had given, make good use of it, and sell back to us what they produced. Few considered that we might have a different point of view.

As just one indicator of this benign blindness, I still get astonished when I pick up a textbook on world drama, say, and find a thousand pages devoted to drama in the West and perhaps three to the East—one for Sanskrit theater, one for Japanese, and one for Chinese, each of which has a tradition at least as old as that of English drama.

This situation is slowly being balanced, but it still sorrows me to see how little awareness there is in the West of the culture and concerns of the rest of the world. Recently I was looking at a multi-volume diary covering the years 1945 to 1962, written by a well-known political commentator in London, to see what he had to say about events in India. Gandhi's name didn't even appear in the index.

Such observations explain why I appreciate the work of the historian Arnold Toynbee. "What I am trying to do," he said once, "is to explain to the West that we are only a small minority in the world." With remarks like this, we Asians became ardent fans. On one occasion, when Toynbee spoke in the city of Madras, he drew probably the largest audience of his career.

It was while he was walking about among the ruins of Greece and Crete, Toynbee said, that great questions began to rise in his mind. Why should such monumental civilizations suffer such a torturous decline? That is the question he tried to answer in his exhaustive *Study of History*. The inspiration came to him while he was on the Orient Express, watching those storied Thracian landscapes flee past. In his unconscious, a plan for history was taking shape.

The outcome appeared in twelve volumes, more than

three million words, which took him forty years of dedicated work. The book is not just a recording of facts and figures. It is an interpretation of history, and whether we agree with it or not, it is even more thought-provoking today than when it first appeared. Toynbee asks in detail, Why did twenty-six great civilizations fall? And his conclusion: Because they could not change their direction, their way of thinking, to meet the changing challenges of life.

This is a spiritual question, not just an intellectual exercise or a matter of physical resources. Its relevance came out in an arresting sentence in the interview he gave the London *Sunday Observer* on the occasion of his eighty-fifth birthday: "Man's plundering of nature now threatens him with pollution and depletion." What he is hinting at is that ours may become the twenty-seventh civilization to wither. Toynbee, like the great mystics, harbored an abiding faith in the spiritual regeneration of mankind. Yet without this regeneration, he saw almost no chance of our survival as a civilization.

Destroyer of Evil

SHARVA

Ordinarily this is a name of Shiva, though it appears as a name of Vishnu as well—a reminder that we all worship the same Godhead, whatever name we use.

My ancestral family, incidentally, built two temples near our home, one to Sri Krishna and one to Shiva. This is unusual, for generally people worship one or the other but not both. The big joke among the neighbors was that the Eknath family likes to butter its bread on both sides. "We're taking no chances," we used to reply. "Who knows who will be seated on the throne on Judgment Day?"

Sharva draws an image from archery again: it comes from the word *sharu,* "arrow." The mantram is an arrow we can use to shoot down any negative emotion or selfish desire, and ultimately hit the target of Self-realization.

The Inexhaustible
Treasure

NIDHIR-AVYAYA

Awareness of God is a rare kind of treasure: the more you draw on it, the more you will have. This aspect of Self-realization should appeal to high-powered business types. The more patient you are with people, the more patience you will have. The more generous you are to-day, the more generosity you will have tomorrow. The more love you give, the more loving you become. It's a strange paradox, perhaps the best-kept banking secret in all of life.

Remember those great words of Jesus: "To those who have, more shall be given; from those who lack, even the little they have will be taken away." The principle can be stated in the plainest of terms: if you are selfish, stingy with your love, the scant security you cling to will be battered to pieces by life. But if you give of yourself freely, without any thought of personal reward, your security will grow unshakable; you will always have more to give.

Being

Thousands of years ago the Upanishads posed a penetrating question: "When life leaves the body, what remains?" The words are so simple that it takes a while for the implications to sink in. This whole complicated mechanism that we call our body and mind is dead equipment when life leaves us. It is like a Porsche whose driver has abandoned it because it ran out of gas, like a house whose owner has forgotten where it is.

Being, this name suggests, is something that the body "contains." As Sri Ramakrishna used to say, just as the sword rests in its scabbard, the arrow in its quiver, so the soul, pure existence, rests in the body-mind-sense-intellect complex.

Ramakrishna liked to compare the layers of this complex to a coconut, which has a smooth outer rind and a fibrous middle layer surrounding the husk and white flesh. The vast majority of us, Ramakrishna said, are like green coconuts, which feel very heavy because the shell, the kernel, and everything inside are stuck together and cannot be separated.

When a coconut is ripe, however, the insides dry a little, and the kernel pulls free from the husk and rattles around. A skillful cook has only to shake a coconut to find out if it is ripe. It will feel light, and you will hear the kernel knocking about inside. Such a coconut can be used to make hundreds of luscious things.

Those who have learned to identify with the Self,

Ramakrishna says, are like ripe coconuts: detached. They never once identify themselves with their container, the body. They are not held by anything: no selfish ties, no purely personal urges. They are free.

The Highway
of the Free

MUKTANAM PARAMAGATI

This word "free," *mukta,* is related to the word *moksha,* which means freedom or liberation in the spiritual sense. This is the freedom we are really looking for: not the freedom to do as we please whenever we please, but freedom from the limitations of self-centered conditioning that tie us down. These limitations make us into chickens, scratching at the ground to look for a few crumbs of pleasure and profit. We should be like eagles, Saint Teresa of Avila says, soaring in the sky.

The other day in a bookstore I saw an intriguing title: *The Handbook of Knots*—a complete manual for tying all kinds of knots, from useful to decorative, very stylishly produced. I wanted to suggest to the proprietor that my little book *Meditation* would sit perfectly on the same shelf, for meditation is the art of *untying* knots.

In today's tense world, most of us have nights when we go to bed and can't sleep because our shoulder or neck is knotted up. Similarly, there are knots in the mind, and they produce much the same kind of effect but farther-reaching. It is these knots in the mind that make life frustrating and unsatisfying. In meditation we work at loosening these knots and finally untying them altogether, and each one undone means a release of vital energy.

Support

If you can reach deep into your consciousness to rest on the Lord, you will have all the support you need to face anything in the world of experience. On the other hand, most of us have little connection with this divine support, so we lack the security necessary to face even one hostile person. Without some awareness that the Self is within us, the same Self in all, it is natural to get agitated, resentful, or afraid.

Mahatma Gandhi says memorably:

> I have been a willing slave to this most exacting Master for more than half a century. His voice has been increasingly audible as the years have rolled by. He has never forsaken me even once in my darkest hour. He has saved me often even against myself and left me not a vestige of independence. The greater the surrender to him, the greater has been my joy.

Lord of the World

Hindu stories sometimes like to have a little fun with some of the gods and goddesses in which the Lord is worshipped so devoutly. These stories have a subtle way of showing something of the divine paradox at the bottom of life. How, for example, could Krishna, the divine master of the universe, be born and grow up more or less like any other child, getting in trouble, playing tricks on his mother, and having fun with his chums?

In one of the marvelous stories about baby Krishna, his mother gets anxious because her little one has been eating sand. She grabs him by the hand and pries open his mouth. But when she peers inside, she sees the entire cosmos there within that tiny mouth. Awestruck, she goes into ecstasy. When she finally returns to ordinary consciousness, Sri Krishna draws a veil over her mind again, so that she can still relate to this cosmic child as her son.

This gives a valuable insight as to how to deal with our own children. First, we have to remember to treat them with the utmost love all the time. We have to remember their needs before everybody else's. In many ways children are closer to divinity than we adults are. On the other hand, we need to be practical: while their core is divine, their outer crust need not be so.

The Son of Man

This very ancient name is a patronymic of the word *nara*, which means "man." So Narayana means, roughly, "son of man," or perhaps "he who is the resting place of man." "Man" here means human being, and this name reminds us that we can find our cure only in him, our rest only in her, if we think of God as the Divine Mother. Narayana is the resting place of all.

The name Narayana in itself is an ancient mantram, and it also appears in the longer mantram *Om Namo Narayanaya*, "Om, I worship Narayana." Narayana is also a rather popular name for boys. It is very, very common in our Hindu tradition to give children a holy name. Millions of boys are called Rama, and millions of girls are called Sita. I even had one cousin who was called Shivaramakrishna. This is a useful custom, for it means that the household is alive with the Holy Name. Even if the younger children are quarreling, it is still "Hey, Rama, you have my toy!" and "You're wrong, Radha, it's mine!"

There is a famous story in our scriptures about a rich merchant whose son's name was Narayana. This proved very fortunate for that merchant, because he was a rather greedy man—in fact, he was so selfishly attached to his wealth that he had very little love left over to give to anything else. Only his son Narayana was important to him, perhaps even more than his money.

As this merchant got older he came to be more and more of a misanthrope, never wanting to see anyone but his accountants, staying all day in his storeroom counting his money. The only exception was Narayana, whom he welcomed at all times.

Finally, while his son was away on a business errand, the old man fell deathly ill. He lay on his deathbed waiting for the end, bitterly resenting the fact that he would soon have to leave behind everything he had so carefully and compulsively hoarded. But most of all he yearned to see his son. And at the very last moment, as death claimed him, he forgot all about his money and his possessions and called out with all his heart, "Narayana! *Narayana!*"

In a moment Yama, the King of Death, appeared to claim the old man's soul. But then something very strange happened: the Lord, Vishnu, also appeared. "What are you doing here?" Yama protested. "You know this man was no saint."

"I know," the Lord agreed, "but I had to come. He called my name with all his heart."

"Don't worry about that," said Yama, relieved. "He wasn't calling *you*. Narayana is his son."

"That doesn't matter. He called my name with devotion with his dying breath, and whoever calls on me like that, I can't refuse."

So the wealthy merchant won on a technicality.

The Supreme Godhead

Brahman comes from the root *brih,* "to expand." This is the divine nature of reality, and when I read about the theory of the expanding universe, I get fascinated by the applications it has for understanding the concept of Brahman.

Black holes today have become a conversation piece. Once the vogue was to talk about existentialism; now it is, "Did you know that black holes have negative mass?" or "Have you heard the latest joke about black holes?" One prominent South Indian astrophysicist says that when he was in the hospital, the nurses kept asking him to explain about black holes.

One lesson of the black hole is that matter can be so infinitely concentrated that it vanishes in a "null point," a "singularity" where an immense amount of matter takes up no space at all. The "Big Bang" theory postulates that the universe was born in a kind of cosmic explosion from such a point—literally everything out of nothing. In the language of Hinduism and Buddhism this is *mahamaya,* the power that brings the universe—matter and energy, time and space—out of "seed form" and keeps it expanding for eons, until someday expansion will cease and the cosmos will gradually collapse into itself again.

This gives a small clue to the nature of Brahman. Brahman cannot be grasped intellectually. The supreme reality cannot be described. All we can do is to concentrate our love and devotion on those great manifestations of

Brahman which have appeared in all major religious traditions, such as Sri Krishna, the Compassionate Buddha, and Jesus the Christ.

The Manifestation
of Brahman

BRAHMANYA

In Hinduism the Godhead takes human form as an *avatara,* from *ava,* "down," and *tri,*"to come"—a divine incarnation. But this name also refers to the Self that is within all of us. The Upanishads say simply, *Tat tvam asi*: "Thou art That." The supreme reality is our real Self, and when we discover this truth for ourselves, we attain complete fulfillment and abiding joy. As Saint Bernard explains in simple words,

> For my part, I think the chief reason which prompted
> the invisible God to become visible in the flesh and to
> hold converse with human beings was to lead physical men
> and women, who are only able to love physically, to the
> healthy love of his physical form, and afterwards, little
> by little, to spiritual love.

Maker of Reality

Once, when I was teaching meditation on the Berkeley campus, I went with friends into a coffee house on Telegraph Avenue and as soon as we sat down, the party at the next table launched a highly abstract discussion about levels of reality, about being and becoming. They may have thought that is the kind of talk a meditation teacher likes to hear. Actually, what reality boils down to is respecting all. It is as simple as that.

However, though this may be simple, it is often not clear to us in the million and one details of the day, generally because we are preoccupied with ourselves. When we make somebody wait unnecessarily, we are not showing respect: our actions say clearly, "My time is more important than yours." When we avoid somebody we don't like, we are not showing them respect, even if we think they won't notice. And when we get offended because somebody hasn't taken proper notice of us, we are not showing respect for ourselves.

I have become so sensitive to this matter of respect that it sometimes makes my wife laugh at how far I go. The other morning I was seated at breakfast and enjoying some muffins prepared painstakingly by Laurel, when I noticed our dog Ganesha sitting outside patiently waiting for a snack. "You finish your muffins," Christine said, "and then take care of him." But I find I am unable to do that. I treat Ganesha exactly as I would treat a young fellow who has dropped in on me: I feel hospitable. I went out and shared a muffin with him, then came back and finished my breakfast in peace. It's not just that it pleases Ganesha; this is something I owe to myself. I would have felt small if I had made him wait for me to finish.

On the other hand, we need artistry and a sense of appropriateness to carry this out; that is why I am stressing the mental state involved—the mind rather than the muffin. For example, I don't invite Ganesha to come sit at the table with us, and I don't go overboard and have nice shirts and trousers made for him either. I have seen dogs dressed in chic fashions, and I am sure the owners thought they were putting their pets first. The dogs themselves probably had different ideas! It is good to respect the Lord in all creatures, but we also need to use our common sense.

This call to respect all life is an inspiration for us to expand our consciousness. When we get caught up in one person, however pleasant and affectionate the relationship may be, our consciousness is narrowed down to just a slit; we have room for that person, but no one else will fit. That is why I appeal to everybody to seek out others' company, to be sociable with everybody, to spend time working and relaxing with other people. If you are meditating sincerely and following all the allied disciplines, consciousness will expand; your respect will grow broader and deeper.

The Creator

The last *a* of this name is long, to distinguish *Brahma* from *Brahman*. Brahman is the attributeless Godhead, of which all the deities in the Hindu pantheon are expressions; Brahma is the Creator in the Hindu trinity, as Vishnu is the Preserver and Shiva the Destroyer.

As far as my knowledge goes, there is no temple for Brahma anywhere in India. This is an interesting comment on the Hindu outlook. The significance of this omission is profound: it means that we haven't exactly come into a higher state of consciousness by being born here on earth.

Most of us seem to believe just the opposite. From the way the world behaves, we seem to believe that human birth represents a great improvement in our state of being—that we have come from a really unsuitable place and have happily found ourselves transferred to a much more advantageous location. No Hindu would agree with this. We feel much more at home with the Christian mystics' assertion: that all of us come from God, and to God we shall return. This interim period is a kind of exile, a wandering in some alien land; until we discover the Lord in our own heart, so that we live in God every moment, we can never feel quite at home with this life on earth.

East and West, there have been many mystics to go to the other extreme, describing life as the "valley of the shadow of death." This is not my point of view, but there

277

is truth in it, and the message spelled out so clearly in Saint Teresa's lines rings in my ears always: "Everything passes; God alone never changes." Just see how soon each week passes, how quickly each weekend comes. And with it, each of us has moved one week closer to the great change called death. This may seem a grim reminder, but it is one that all of us should keep before our eyes always. It gives meaning to every moment, throws everything in life into perspective.

Who Makes
Reality Increase

This name comes from the root *vardh,* "to increase, to spread." It is a reminder that each of us has the responsibility of spreading love and increasing others' happiness. There was an emperor in ancient India with a similar name, which I like very much: Harshavardhana, "he whose joy lies in increasing the joy of his people."

To me, it is an axiom by now that nobody can win even happiness by inflicting pain on others. No matter how much satisfaction you think you can get by being discourteous to somebody who has wronged you, I assure you it will never happen, because that is the law of karma. If you give joy, you will receive joy; if you inflict pain, you will receive pain. The choice is ours.

When I see people fishing, for example, I cannot understand how anybody can get pleasure out of inflicting pain on those poor creatures. It goes without saying that I feel the same about hunting, whatever justification is offered. "Deer season" to me doesn't mean it is time to kill deer. For me it means a time to show films about deer, to write stories about deer, to make people sensitive to our kinship with these gentle creatures in every possible way. The deer in our ashram are so trustful now that if we come across one grazing, we have to walk around; the creature won't bother to move. I have even thought of carrying a little brush in my pocket to give their fur a brushing. That is my deer season.

The other day, as we were driving over the creek on our way into town, I spotted a turtle having a snooze near the edge of the pavement. People may not see him there, I said to myself, and they might run over him by accident. So I asked the driver to stop while we picked him up and found a safer spot for his siesta.

To live up to the ideal suggested by *Brahmavivardhana,* we have to spread love everywhere through our personal contact with people and creatures. You will come to feel toward every girl or boy exactly as you would toward your own children. This doesn't take away from your love for your children; it means you gain the same love for other children as well. And they all respond to it, too.

Wisdom

VEDA

The word *Veda* comes from the root *vid,* "to know." The Vedas are the most ancient scriptures to come down to us from the ancient seers of India. They are held to be the sacred word of the eternal, breathed forth at the beginning of time to guide the world to its ultimate goal, the return to eternal Being at the end of time.

It is not without a touch of humor that the Lord is called Veda. It is a little like saying Mr. Scripture. The Veda is the scripture that embodies the eternal wisdom, and the Lord is the personification of that wisdom. In India this wisdom flows in an unbroken stream of sacred works: from the Veda into the Upanishads, from the Upanishads into the Bhagavad Gita, and from the Gita out into many, many channels in the works of Vedanta and Yoga and other schools and traditions. In a sense, all this is the Veda: all eternal wisdom that we can verify in our own consciousness in meditation.

Knower of Reality

Brahmavid is "knower of the supreme"; *brahmavidya* is "the supreme education." That is how the Hindu scriptures refer to meditation, where instead of enrolling in the courses of a professor from Harvard, you get the best professor in the world: your own Self. The Self has degrees from every galaxy in the universe, and those who study with him sincerely do not have to produce transcripts or diplomas or references. Their personal example of love and wisdom establishes their credentials, and through these they pass to others their knowledge of the Self.

True education, in other words, is not so much stuffing knowledge in as drawing wisdom out. The Self is the knower of wisdom because he is the source. This is not just theory. The Self is pure intelligence, pure consciousness, the very principle of knowing. The mind and intellect are inert without the Self; they are only his instruments. When these instruments are purified in meditation, concentration becomes as penetrating as a laser, bringing the learning capacity of genius to whatever field you take up. That is why meditation is what William James called "education *par excellence.*"

One of the best definitions of education I have heard comes, I think, from an Oxford don: the main purpose of education is to enable you to know when somebody is talking rot. Even where experts are gathered, I need hardly tell you, wisdom and discrimination are not always abundant. An expert can get caught in his own tiny groove and forget that there is much more to the world all around him. In the rest of life, experts are just like the rest of us. No field is really isolated. The questions that matter in every field are tied to the rest of life, on which we and the experts stand on equal ground.

This name of the Lord is a reminder that every one of us has the same source of wisdom within. In the Gita, Sri Krishna asks, "Who do you think is the real author of the Vedas? Vyasa? I just engaged Vyasa as a brilliant ghost-writer, to put into verse what I inspired in him." Vyasa gets the credit because even in ancient India it was hard to find someone who is a good Sanskrit scholar and can put ideas into meter on the spot. Instead of Sri Krishna sitting in a big executive chair with Vyasa taking shorthand, imagine Sri Krishna seated inside Vyasa, dictating the Vedas in his meditation. That is what inspiration means.

To get this kind of divine inspiration, all we need to do is still the mind, quieten self-will, put the intellect to sleep with a local anesthetic for a while, and ask the senses to go climb a tree. Then we will be able to hear the eternal wisdom that is the Self.

Desire

Our real desire in life, as the Bible puts it, is to love the Lord with all our heart, all our mind, all our spirit, and all our strength. The human being's infinite capacity to desire can never be fulfilled by anything less.

Unfortunately, it is equally part of the human condition to believe that we can fulfill our need to love and to be loved by grasping at things and people. When we search outside like this for fulfillment, we misuse our power to love. When we clutch at or cling to anything other than God, we are denying the very possibility of love.

In his *Confessions,* Saint Augustine gives a very different idea of love. This is the same Augustine who in his early life explored the entire gamut of pleasure. He speaks from his own life when he compares spiritual fulfillment to the ordinary pleasures he had enjoyed before:

> Not the beauty of any bodily thing, nor the order of the seasons, not the brightness of light that rejoices the eye, nor the sweet melodies of all songs, nor the sweet fragrance of flowers and ointments and spices: not manna nor honey, not the limbs that carnal love embraces. None of these things do I love in loving my God. Yet in a sense I do love light and melody and fragrance and food and embrace when I love my God—the light and the voice and the fragrance and the food and embrace in the soul, when that light shines upon my soul which no place can contain, and that

voice sounds which no time can take from me; when I
breathe that fragrance which no wind scatters, and eat the
food which is not lessened by eating, and lie in the embrace
which satiety never comes to sunder. This it is that I love
when I love my God.

Our ordinary conception of joy is limited to a few bits
of sensory pleasure, which we hold on to with a fierce
tenacity that enslaves us. But the suspicion that joy
comes from within us brings a new sense of freedom. No
longer compulsively driven by personal desire—for
money or possessions, prestige or pleasure or power—we
begin to exercise choices where we never dreamed
choices could be made.

Destroyer
of Selfish Craving

Kama here means any selfish desire. Often the word is translated as sexual desire, but that is a little misleading. Kama is any private pleasure—something that I want to enjoy just for myself, no matter what the cost to others. It can be any compulsive craving—for food, or alcohol, or drugs, or even power or fame. Only when we are free from such compulsions can we know what a thorn in our flesh kama is, and what a blessing it is to be free from all selfish craving.

It is the nature of a compulsion to be almost beyond control. As long as we are in the grip of the desire, it seems we cannot think of anything else until we satisfy it. Overeating is a familiar example. We may know that a hot fudge sundae means calories we don't need, but the desire has a hold on us and we say this is what we want. Not until we have eaten the sundae, after the clamor of the desire quiets down, can we listen to the voice that reminds us we have made a mistake.

The important point here is not that there is anything wrong in eating a sundae, but simply that we do not have the capacity to choose when it is all right and when it isn't. For hot fudge sundae we can all make our own substitutions. Some of these compulsive desires are not too harmful in themselves, but when this inability to exercise our power to choose extends to smoking or drinking or drugs, we begin to cause serious suffering to ourselves and those around us.

One painful compulsion not infrequently occurs in personal relationships, when we clutch at our friends or partner for support. This leads to all kinds of trouble. When we are grasping at another person, the real tragedy is that we cease to see that person. He or she becomes merely an object for propping ourselves up, which is an open invitation to jealousy and finally to a broken relationship. People with this kind of problem simply go from one relationship to another, always grasping and always missing what they are grasping for. Unfortunately, they cannot see what the problem is because they have lost the power to choose.

The major cause of all these kinds of compulsions is obsessive identification with the body. That the sun takes its bath in the sea at night, as many people in my village used to believe, is a very small superstition compared to the superstition that we are the body. It is because we identify ourselves with the body that when a sensory craving comes, we feel we have no choice but to satisfy it. The alternative is to feel frustrated, repressed, and unfulfilled.

It never occurs to us that we might not be our desires. But as long as we identify ourselves with our desires, we can never be masters of ourselves. And to be masters of ourselves means that we must be able to *choose* what we desire, choose what we think: which means that for many, many years we will have to say no to a lot of compulsive thoughts and cravings.

When you are trying to resist a harmful desire, one helpful clue is to remember that the real source of that desire is not the body but the mind. Often, for example, I see people in ice cream parlors who are in no need of nourishment. The emptiness they feel inside them is not a physical emptiness, but they interpret it physically because they identify themselves with the body. Similarly, when we smoke we are simply punishing the body for the restlessness of the mind. This is why physical approaches to these problems can never be of much help in overcoming a destructive habit.

Once you can trace a desire to the mind, you get some detachment from it. The desire loses some of its urgency, and when the pressure of desire is relieved, we can remember what we know from previous experience: that most desires are not very long-lasting. An hour ago we may have wanted a hot fudge sundae, but now what we really want is a piece of baklava. In another sixty minutes our all-encompassing desire will be to fly to the Greek islands for some ouzo. So one helpful tip for resisting a desire is simply to put it off. For all its cleverness, the mind is not difficult to trick. If it asks for baklava now, just tell it to wait until you have finished reading this book. By that time, the chances are that you will have forgotten the baklava completely.

For the more adventurous, however, an even better method for fighting compulsions is to do just the opposite of what they demand. When all you want to do is lock yourself in your room and spend the day with a favorite novel, that is the time to go out and be with people, especially in doing something that will benefit others. This is a sure test of spiritual growth. When the desire comes to do your own thing, to bask in something you just love, even if it is something harmless, try throwing yourself into a selfless job with energy and enthusiasm. When you can do that, you are really making progress.

Spiritual Teacher

GURU

Guru is a word that has come into the English language to stay, but I suspect that few know its actual significance. *Guru* literally means "heavy." A guru is a person who is very heavy—so heavy that nothing can unsettle his love or push over her patience, no matter what the storms.

In the modern world, very few can claim this stature. Most of us behave like wisps of straw or scraps of paper that can be blown about by any gust of passion. We seem just to react to what others do. If somebody is angry at us, we feel justified in being angry in return. Not at all. Those who are subject to resentment or hostility or retaliation or revenge are not *guru* but *laghu,* light. They have very little weight. If somebody pushes them, they push right back, a little like mechanical dolls.

I think it was in an old film of Charlie Chaplin's that I saw this portrayed. Charlie is being chased by the police for an offense he hasn't committed. He finds it difficult to escape them, so when he passes a merry-go-round, he pretends to be one of the mechanical creatures. At a certain point, all these dolls with sticks start hitting one another. Charlie does just what he sees them doing, and his timing is perfect. The performance is so convincing that the police mistake him for a machine.

This is what we do when we try to "get even"—which to me has always seemed like getting odd. If someone hits me, it is absurd for me to hit them back like a mechanical toy. If someone is rude, it is absurd for me to be annoyed. Where is the connection?

If getting resentful could solve such problems, I would be all for resentment. But it doesn't solve anything; it only tears us apart. It is very hard to accept this, I agree; that is human nature. Here is where the guru is most helpful. By his steadiness and unflappability, he shows us that we can endure the storms of life without unkindness, and actually flourish on stress.

In India, no one in his right mind covets the role of spiritual teacher. It is a very, very difficult job. Everyone knows how difficult it is to solve problems even in one personal relationship, to move closer when things are going wrong. A spiritual teacher has this kind of complication multiplied many times over. Only a person who is completely established in spiritual awareness can safely play this role, and only if he or she has perfect detachment.

When you realize the unity of life, as I said before, it means that others' grief, others' problems, become your own. It means that there are always problems, there is always grief, for someone who has attained Self-realization: not personal problems, but the burdens of those around you. So the role of guru is not free of pain. But this pain is not borne supinely, for those who realize God also have the capacity to relieve the pain of others. It is in this that joy comes—the kind of joy that no money can buy, no pleasure ever bring.

This name of God reminds us that the real spiritual teacher is in all of us—the Lord, our deepest Self. When we feel attracted to a teacher, we are expected to scrutinize his life closely and see that he embodies the highest ideals that all religions teach. Then, if he does, we should give him all our loyalty and all our love; for it is primarily by focusing our love that a spiritual teacher helps us to unify our consciousness.

The teacher too will be watching us, looking to see if we are capable of wholehearted dedication. If we are, the time will come when the teacher says, "You are my student." Then the bond is sealed. The job of the teacher is to take us to samadhi, when we see that our real teacher has always been the Self within us. And our job is to give him, or her, our very best, without any reservations. A ballet master at the Bolshoi demands no less.

The guru's is the highest form of love, the greatest gift that one human being can give to another. In the Hindu tradition it is the guru who inspires all the students who are devoted to him to flood their hearts with the ecstatic love of God, which brings all temptations to an end, dissolves all conflicts, and heals all divisions in consciousness.

A great Sufi saint once said, "I am He whom I love, and He whom I love is I. We are two spirits, dwelling in the same body. If thou seest me, thou seest him; and if thou seest him, thou seest both." This is why in India we go to our sages—Ramana Maharshi, Mahatma Gandhi, Sri Ramakrishna, Anandamayi Ma—simply to look at them. We are not just seeing them; we are seeing through them to the supreme reality, which reminds us that we have the same reality within us too. When we have difficulties, we go to our teacher. We don't even have to talk; it is enough just to look and draw inspiration.

"Evil cannot overcome an illumined man, because he overcomes evil. Sin cannot burn an illumined woman, because she burns out sin." This is what the Upanishads said about the illumined teacher. That is why going to a God-conscious man or woman helps us to overcome evil in ourselves. Our love is an open door for the teacher's love and wisdom to reach in, dissolving little by little the negative compulsions that have caused so much trouble in the past.

The Holy Name

The Lord is always with us in the Holy Name. He *is* the mantram. So when we use the mantram regularly, it becomes a way of calling the Lord collect. We don't need to know all his thousand names. We can just say *Rama, Rama, Rama,* or *Jesus, Jesus, Jesus*; he will get the message.

The Lord has a thousand names, a thousand hands, a thousand faces: that is to say, his names and forms are endless. Robert, Ellen, Rick, Kate, Claudia, Jim, are all names of the Lord, because he is present in everyone. This is not just a philosophical statement, it is very personal and practical. If we see this, we can never lose respect for anyone. More important, we will never lose faith. This is the marvelous result of the universal vision: we never lose our faith that everybody is capable of revealing the Lord within.

The Lord is the name behind all names, the face behind all faces. This is the realization that samadhi brings. The world is full of God. After samadhi we don't see just the external appearance of life. We penetrate deep into life, and with that same penetration we see the Lord in everybody, all the time. As the Upanishads say, some people have two feet, others (like our dog Ganesha) happen to have four feet; but in all of them dwells the same Lord. In this realization of the One, through the One, with the One comes the beginning of endless love.

When we study these names of the Lord, I would like to repeat, we are not just unearthing old Sanskrit words, however beautiful they may be. These are not mere names. They are marvelous concepts which throw light on how to live: long, healthy, secure, joyful lives, not in seclusion but in a world full of problems. When you reflect on these thousand names of the Lord of Love, who is enshrined in the depths of our consciousness, try to apply them in all your activities. Then each Holy Name can help to improve the quality of your daily life.

The Lord is present in all, so everybody's name is his. He is also beyond all, so he has no name at all. But for me his name is Krishna, whom I find the perfect expression of God's love and beauty. In our Hindu scriptures we have a story of how Krishna got his name. Sri Krishna's mother was spending sleepless nights trying to think of suitable names. Finally, she decides to leave the choice up to a great sage, but when the baby is born and she takes him and puts him on the sage's lap, the sage asks, "What name shall I give him who already has a thousand names?" Finally they settle on Krishna.

Until we attain illumination, we need to repeat our mantram as often and as sincerely as we can. Whatever name we choose—*Krishna, Rama, Jesus, Hail Mary,* or any other sacred formula that has come down to us in the great religious traditions of the world—without constant repetition in the mind, it is not likely to penetrate the depths of the heart. Mira, the great woman saint of medieval India, said that without the holy name, living is in vain. You may be eating, you may be drinking, you may be having a good time, you may be making money, but if you don't repeat God's name, you are living in vain. Without the mantram, Mira says, life is like a temple without a lamp, like a night without the moon, like a meal without salt, like a loving wife when the husband is away, like a tree without leaves, like a pool without water. In all these simple ways she expresses the emptiness of a life without God.

When ecstatic love is awakened in the heart, all this emptiness goes out of our life forever. Repeating the Lord's name then becomes a great joy. To use orthodox language, we worship God whenever we repeat his name.

But we also worship him when we use kind language under provocation, or when we give our time and energy freely and cheerfully to causes that benefit the world. We are worshipping when we meditate regularly, or when we control our senses when they want to go after some harmful pleasure. Then our whole life becomes an offering of love. This is the real spiritual life, where, as Sri Ramakrishna says, we make merry in the mansion of God, seeing and serving the Lord in all.

Thousand Names
of Vishnu

This is a translation of the portion of the Anushasana Parva
of the *Mahabharata* known as *Vishnusahasranama,* the
"Thousand Names of Vishnu." Translating these names
into English is a rather difficult undertaking, in part because
there may be several meanings for each Sanskrit word, with
the context giving the clue as to which meaning is the main
one and which meanings are only hinted at. Very often the
Sanskrit poets played upon these multiple meanings, using
the secondary meanings as an artful poetic device. In translation, of course, only one meaning of each name can be
conveyed, so a good deal of the richness is lost. Also, there
are puns and what almost seem to be riddles in the Sanskrit
that cannot be rendered into English.

He is the universe and pervades all as Lord Vishnu.
He is the mystic syllable used in the ritual,
Lord of past, present, and future,
The maker and supporter of all that is.
He is Being and the Self in every creature;
He is the essence of all beings. [1]

He is the pure and supreme Self.
He is the highway of the free.
He changes not.
He is Spirit; he is the witness;
He knows all fields of knowledge and perishes not. [2]

He is yoga and leads those who know yoga.
He rules spirit and matter.
He has taken the form of the man-lion.
He is beautiful and is called Keshava.
He is the supreme Person. [3]

He is all.
He is Shiva, armed with an arrow.
He is the firmly fixed beginning of all beings.
He is an inexhaustible treasure.
He is existence, the cause and the support.
He is the origin and the power.
He is the Lord. [4]

He is self-existent and bestows eternal peace.
He is the child of the infinite, with eyes like the lotus.
He is the cosmic sound, without beginning or end.
He is the ordainer and the bestower.
He is the firm foundation of all things. [5]

He cannot be measured.
He thrills with joy and a lotus blooms from his navel.
Lord of the immortals, he can do all things.
He is the first man and the best craftsman,
The strongest and the oldest;
He is constant like the polestar. [6]

He cannot be understood.
He is Krishna, the Eternal.
He is the destroyer, with reddish eyes;
He is abundant, and the majesty of the thunderbolt is his.
He purifies and he is the highest blessing. [7]

He rules and gives life;
He is life itself.
He is the eldest and the best.
He has created the worlds from the golden egg.
He is the womb of the cosmos.
His ancestor is Madhu and he has slain the demon. [8]

He is the wide-striding Lord who wields the bow.
He is wise and courageous.
He orders the ranks and there is none higher than he.
He is dangerous, grateful, skillful, and self-possessed. [9]

He is lord of the gods.
He is the refuge, the shelter.
He is the seed of all and the birth of progeny.
He is the day and the year.
He is mischievous.
He is certainty and he sees all. [10]

He is the unborn who rules all.
He is fulfilled and has all supernatural powers.
He is the beginning of all and he stands firm.
He is the sun and his soul cannot be measured.
All yoga has come forth from him. [11]

He is benevolent and his mind is full of wealth.
He is truth, the soul of equanimity.
He cannot be measured and is impartial;
He does not fail.
His eyes are like the lotus blossom;
His deeds are good and manly. [12]

He is Rudra, of tawny color.
His heads are a multitude.
He is the womb of all and his fame shines brightly.
He is immortal, eternally fixed.
He is the great ascetic who rides an excellent mount. [13]

He travels to all places and knows all.
He is the brightness of the sun.
His armies march everywhere, stirring up the people.
He is the sacred text and knows the sacred wisdom.
He is without arms or legs; his limbs are the Veda.
He is a poet and knower of the Veda. [14]

He oversees the worlds, the gods, and dharma.
He is what is done and what is left undone.

He has four souls, manifested as four.
His arms and teeth are four. [15]

He is the radiant one,
Enjoyment and enjoyer;
He is the patient first-born of the world.
Without sin, he is both victory and victor.
He is the womb and he restores what is lost. [16]

He is the younger Indra,
Yet his strength surpasses Indra's.
Though a dwarf, he is tall.
He does not err and is pure.
He is the totality from which creation flows.
He is firm restraint and the controller called death. [17]

He is the one to be known.
He is a healer and a slayer of heroes.
His meditation does not waver.
He comes in the sweet season of spring.
He is beyond the knowing of the senses.
He is the great magician.
His vigor is great, as is his might. [18]

He holds up the mountain.
Great is his wisdom, great his courage;
Mighty are his power and splendor.
His form of great beauty can never be known;
His essence can never be measured. [19]

He is the great archer.
He carries the earth and is the home of Sri.
He is the good way, and his will cannot be resisted.
He delights the gods.
He is the cowherd and leads the cowherd boys. [20]

He is the sun's rays.
He is subdued.
He is the swan and the eagle,
The cosmic serpent and the cosmic womb.

He brings good from suffering.
From his lotus womb he creates all beings. [21]

He is deathless and sees all.
He is a lion and the one who brings all together.
He is found at the union of day and night.
He is unborn, immovable, a teacher hard to bear.
He is widely praised and slays the enemies of the gods. [22]

He is the guru and the best of spiritual teachers.
He is our home and he is truth.
His courage is born of truth.
He is as the twinkling of the eye but never blinks.
He wears a garland and is the master of words.
His thoughts are noble. [23]

He has gone at the beginning.
He is the lord of the village.
Great good fortune is his.
He is logic.
He leads and he fans the wind.
His heads are a multitude and he is the Self in all.
His eyes and feet cannot be numbered. [24]

He is the revolving of the heavens.
He is detached from the world and he is hidden.
He tramples the worlds.
He is today.
He rolls up the worlds at the end of time.
He is fire and the unsleeping wind.
He carries the burden of the earth. [25]

He is gracious and serene.
He holds all together and enjoys all.
He is mighty and a doer of good acts.
He does what is good and is good.
He is the sage who fathered the Ganges.
He is man and the son of man. [26]

He cannot be counted or measured.
He is distinguished from all others.

He follows the rules and is pure.
His purpose and intentions are accomplished.
He grants and is the means to the ultimate goal. [27]

He is the male serpent and the bull.
He is called Vishnu.
He has the limbs and strength of a bull.
He gives prosperity and he prospers.
He is solitary,
The ocean of eternal wisdom. [28]

Beautiful are his arms and irresistible.
He is eloquent, a great lord, generous and benevolent.
Many and mighty are his forms.
Emanating light, he shines forth. [29]

He holds strength, majesty, and glory.
His soul is revealed in light and he burns.
He waxes with the clearly spoken holy word.
He is the Holy Name.
He is the rays of the moon and the light of the sun. [30]

He is the rising of the moon and he is the sun;
He is the mark of the hare seen in the moon.
He the lord of the gods and the healing herb.
He is the bridge between the worlds,
And the bold advance of truth and justice. [31]

He is the lord of what has been, what will be, and what is.
He purifies like the wind and he is air and fire.
He destroys selfish craving and fashions desire.
He is desirable and he is desire;
He is the lord who gives what is desired. [32]

He made time begin and he keeps it turning.
Many are his stratagies and illusions.
Great is his appetite.
Though difficult to see, yet he has a manifest form.
He has conquered endless thousands. [33]

He is the one whom we desire but he is not separate from us.
He is the chosen ideal of the learned.
He wears a crest.
He was the father of King Yayati of old.
He foments anger and brings it to an end.
He is the doer, with many arms.
He carries the earth. [34]

He is undiminished and his fame is proclaimed forever.
He is vital energy and he gives vitality.
Born later than Indra,
He is the resting place of the ocean.
He is never careless and never leaves his post. [35]

He is Skanda and he sustains the commander of the gods.
He carries our burdens and grants our prayers.
He carries the wind.
He is the son of Vasudeva and he sheds great light.
He is Indra, first among gods. [36]

He is free from sorrow.
He is the safe passage and the savior.
He is the hero and the son of heroes.
He is kindly and wears a hundred curls.
His consort is the Lotus Goddess;
His eyes are like the lotus flower. [37]

A lotus blooms from his navel and he is lotus-eyed.
A lotus is his womb and he is born in bodily form.
He is great good fortune and he prospers.
He is old and his eyes are large.
On his banner he has the eagle, Garuda. [38]

He cannot be weighed.
He is born of the lion and the elephant.
He inspires fear and accepts all sacrifices equally.
He is the oblation and he removes evil.
He is marked with all auspicious marks.
He is the husband of Lakshmi, goddess of good fortune.
He is unconquered in battle. [39]

He is immutable and he is the reddish sun.
He is the path and the cause.
He has been tied at the middle, yet he prevails.
He carries the vast earth; great good fortune is his.
He is impetuous and his appetites immoderate. [40]

From him arise all creatures, and he stirs them with desire.
He is the shining Spirit and the blessed womb.
He is the supreme Lord.
He is the abyss and that which is hidden.
He is action and its cause.
He creates and he destroys.[41]

He is determination and perseverance.
He is the dwelling and he gives each a place.
He is the unmoving northern star.
He is the highest wealth and is supreme.
He has become manifest and he is content.
He thrives and his eyes are bright. [42]

He is Rama, Prince of Peace, and he is rest.
He is free from craving, and the track to be followed;
He is wise policy, yet he can mislead.
He is the warrior, the strongest of the strong.
He is the eternal law,
And the first among those who follow the law. [43]

Heaven is his home, for he is eternal Spirit.
He is life and he gives life.
He is OM, the cosmic sound
He extends in all directions.
He is the golden seed and the slayer of enemies.
He is the wide-reaching wind and he is born below. [44]

He is the cycling of the seasons and good to look at.
He is time, the supreme, which takes possession of all.
He is fierce and he is the year.
He is skillful, at his ease, and clever in all things. [45]

He is diffused in all directions, yet he stands still.
He stands firm and is the measure.

He is the immortal seed.
He is meaning and the lack of meaning.
He is precious and a great treasure,
And great is his share. [46]

He does not grow weary and his strength is firm.
He is the unborn, the place of sacrifice, a great sacrifice.
He is the polestar and governs the constellations.
He is eager, yet patient as the earth. [47]

He is the sacrifice and the one who is worshipped.
He is the recipient of the rite and the time of sacrifice.
He is the great sacrifice and the way chosen by the good.
He sees all and his soul is free.
He knows all and is the highest wisdom. [48]

His vows are good and his face is good to look on.
He is subtle and his voice is pleasing.
He gives delight and is the best friend.
He captivates the heart and conquers anger.
He has the arms of the hero that rend all asunder. [49]

He gives sleep and he is ruler of himself.
He reaches through all things and he is many.
His deeds are many and he is the years.
He is affectionate and has many dear children.
He has a precious jewel and is the ruler of wealth. [50]

He makes and protects the eternal law of dharma.
He obeys the dharma.
He is truth and the lack of truth.
He is what perishes and what perishes not.
He does not distinguish.
He has fixed the sun with a thousand rays.
He is marked with all good qualities. [51]

He carries the bright discus and abides in goodness.
He is the lion and the lord of all creatures.
He is the first among the gods, the great Lord,
Lord of the gods, their support and elder. [52]

He is the future, the lord of cows and their defender.
He can be reached through wisdom and he is the past.
He sustains the body and is the enjoyer.
He is the leader of the monkeys.
Many rich offerings are given unto him. [53]

He drinks soma and the nectar of immortality.
He is Soma and he overcomes many.
He is first among many.
He is modesty and victory and he keeps his promises.
He is born of the Dasharhas and rules the Satvat clan. [54]

He is the individual soul which lives in the body.
He watches to see whose conduct is fitting.
He is called Mukunda, and his courage is boundless.
He is the ocean and he is without end.
He rests upon the vast ocean and he is death. [55]

He was never born and is worthy of great honor.
He has come to be from his own being.
His enemies have been won over and he is their delight.
He is joy and he brings joy;
He is happy and follows the good law.
He has walked the three wide steps. [56]

He is the great sage, and the teacher Kapila;
He is grateful, the lord of the fertile earth.
He takes three steps and oversees the thirty gods.
He is the great stag.
He brings to fruition the results of action. [57]

He was born as a mighty boar.
He is called Govinda, lord of cows.
His weapons are good and he wears a golden bracelet.
He is secret, profound, a deep wilderness, hidden.
He carries the club and the wheel. [58]

He has created us and he is closer than our own body.
He is invincible.
He is Krishna and the steadfast Balarama;
He is Achyuta and Varuna, and the son of Varuna too.

He is the Tree of Life.
He is haughty, with eyes like the lotus flower. [59]

He is the Lord, full of glory.
He destroys good fortune and brings happiness.
He wears a garland of woodland flowers.
He is armed with a plow and is the son of Aditi.
He is the light of the sun.
He is ever patient and is the very best path. [60]

He carries an excellent bow and wields the axe.
He is violent and he gives wealth.
He is the all-seeing sage Vyasa.
He is the master of speech and was not born of the womb. [61]

Three hymns are sung unto him, and he is the singer;
He is the hymn and he is nirvana.
He is the remedy and the healer.
He has renounced and is at peace;
He is peaceful and is perfect peace;
He is the supreme goal. [62]

His limbs are beautiful and he is the giver of peace.
He has cast forth the worlds.
He is the white lotus and he rests on the lily.
He is good to the cows and leads the cowherds.
He is the defender, with eyes like a bull,
And the cattle are fond of him. [63]

He does not turn back, but his soul has returned.
He reduces all to its essence and gives security.
He is the auspicious one, and his chest
Is marked with the auspicious sign.
He is the dwelling place and the lord of Sri;
Of all those with beauty and good fortune, he is best. [64]

He gives good fortune and is the lord of glory.
He is the home of light and a treasure of riches.
He causes the light to become visible.
He holds and gives glory.

He is the best and he possesses sri.
In all the three worlds he is the last resort. [65]

His eyes and limbs are beautiful.
He is happy and brings delight to many.
He is the lord of the hosts of heavenly lights.
He has conquered himself, yet he is never owned.
He is well known for his goodness.
He has cut away all doubt. [66]

He is elevated and his eyes are everywhere.
He has no lord to rule him and he abides forever.
He rests upon the earth and is its ornament.
He is wealth and he never knows sorrow.
He brings an end to sorrow. [67]

He glows with great brilliance and is much worshipped.
He is in the jar placed for worship.
He is the purifier and the pure Self.
He is Aniruddha and none can stand against him in battle;
He is Pradyumna, a warrior of immeasurable valor. [68]

He has slain Kalanemi and is the hero of the Shura clan,
Lord of the heroes of the Shura family.
He is the Self, and lord of the three worlds.
He is called Keshava and he killed the demon Keshi.
He is Hari, who is the thief. [69]

He is the god of love and gratifies desire.
He is in love and is beloved.
He has fashioned holy tradition.
His form cannot be described.
He is Vishnu and Arjuna, the eternal hero. [70]

He is devoted to Brahman and makes reality.
He is God and the supreme Godhead.
He makes reality increase.
He is the knower of reality and the holy priest.
Possessor of Brahman, knower of Brahman,
He is beloved by the knowers of Brahman. [71]

Vast are his strides, vast his deeds,
Vast is his splendor.
He is the cosmic serpent.
Mighty is his will.
He is the great worshipper;
Great is his sacrifice and great his offering. [72]

He is to be praised always and he is fond of praise.
He is the hymn and the eulogy,
And the one who sings the worship.
He is fond of battle.
He is full and he satisfies.
He is holy and his reputation is pure.
He is without evil. [73]

He is swift as thought and has opened the crossing.
His seed is abundant and he gives abundance.
He gives wealth and is the son of Vasudeva.
He is the bright god and his thoughts are good.
He is the oblation offered at the sacrifice. [74]

His ways are good, as are his deeds.
He is pure goodness and his power is good.
He is the good goal.
He commands the Shura army
He is the best of the Yadu clan.
He is the dwelling place of the good,
And he dwells along the beautiful Yamuna River. [75]

He is the dwelling place of all beings.
He is Krishna, born the son of Vasudeva.
He is the home of all and the god of fire.
He humbles and gives pride, and he is haughty.
He is difficult to bear and verily can never be conquered. [76]

His visage is everywhere and his image is mighty.
As a lamp he shines, yet he is formless.
His forms are many, but he is hidden.
He has hundreds of faces, hundreds of forms. [77]

He is one and he is many;
He is the impulse that brings all to life.
Who is he? What?
He is this and he is that.
He is the goal beyond which there is nothing higher.
He is the kinsman and the lord of the worlds.
He is sweet, and he is fond of his devotees. [78]

His complexion and body are golden in hue.
His body is beautiful.
He wears sandalwood perfume and a beautiful bracelet.
He is the slayer of heroes; there is none like him.
He is empty and desires the butter offering.
He is unmoving, yet he moves. [79]

He is humble, but he gives pride and is worthy of respect.
He is the Lord, who holds together the three worlds.
His thoughts are good and he is born from the sacrifice.
He is wealthy and his thoughts are true.
He holds up the earth. [80]

He is the male seed and carries great splendor.
He is the best of all those who carry weapons.
He is a kind welcome and he is a reprimand.
He is distracted and many-pointed.
He is the elder brother of Gada. [81]

Four are his forms, four his arms,
Four his manifestations, and four his paths.
Four are his selves, four his states of consciousness.
He knows the four Vedas and reduces them to one word. [82]

He has returned home, yet his soul has not withdrawn.
It is hard to win against him, hard to cross him,
Hard to attain him, hard to reach him.
He is a hard passage, a difficult dwelling.
He destroys the wicked foe. [83]

His form is bright, and he can be seen in the peacock.
His thread is beautiful and he makes the web grow.

He is wily and does great things.
He has performed his duty and made his approach. [84]

He is the source and he is beautiful.
He is called Sunda and displays a precious jewel.
His eyes are beautiful. He is the sun.
He has taught the Yajur Veda and he bears a crest.
He is victorious and conquers even the very wise. [85]

He wears a golden mark on his forehead.
He can never be disturbed and is master of eloquence.
He is a deep pool and a vast cave.
He is a great being and a vast treasure. [86]

He is water lily, jasmine, and oleander;
He is rain, wind, and fire.
He drinks the nectar of immortality.
His beauty is deathless.
He knows all things and his face is everywhere. [87]

He is easily obtainable, and easy are his vows.
He is perfect and conquers all opposition.
He burns out his enemies.
He is the banyan, the fig, and the pipal tree.
He has slain Chanura of the Andhra country. [88]

He has a thousand rays and seven tongues.
Seven fuels are offered unto him, and seven are his vehicles.
He is formless, sinless, beyond thought.
He causes and destroys fear. [89]

He is as small as an atom and as large as the universe.
He is thin and he is stout.
He can be described and yet again he cannot.
He is mighty and unrestrained, yet self-controlled.
His mouth pleases.
His family line is ancient and he makes it flourish. [90]

He is a servant, a storyteller, and a yogi.
He is a master of yoga and he gives all longed-for desires.

He is work and toil and he has become thin.
He is the eagle and he carries the wind. [91]

He carries the bow and is a master of archery.
He is government and discipline and the staff that governs.
He is unconquered and patiently bears all things.
He defines but is himself without definition.
He is freedom. [92]

He is courageous, whole and harmonious;
He is truth and is devoted to truth and dharma.
He is loving remembrance and he should be held dear.
He is worthy and he does many kind deeds.
He makes love increase. [93]

His path is in the heavens and he is light.
He enjoys what is good and eats what is offered.
He is all-mighty and he is the sun;
He is the radiant sun-god and the giver of life.
The sun is his eye. [94]

He is without end and the receiver of offerings.
He is the enjoyer, and the giver of happiness.
Many have been his births,
For he was born at the beginning of time.
He has never wearied and has always been forgiving.
He is the great wonder and the foundation of the world. [95]

He is the eternal and the most ancient.
He is the sage Kapila and the unaging monkey Hanuman.
He gives well-being and fashions good fortune.
May it be well with him, the enjoyer of health.
His gifts are good. [96]

He is never angry.
He wears earrings and carries the wheel of the worlds.
He has stepped forth with valor.
His commands cannot be resisted.
He cannot be reached with words, but he is the power of speech.
He is the cool season and has made the wish-giving cow. [97]

He is never unkind and always tender.
He is skillful and straight.
He is the best of those who suffer patiently.
He is fearless and the wisest of the knowing.
Listening to his glory brings grace. [98]

He is the uplifter, and he nips wrong actions in the bud;
He is grace, and brings an end to evil dreams.
He slays the enemy and protects us.
He is the good person and he is life;
He stands all around us. [99]

Endless are his forms, endless his beauty.
He has conquered anger and destroyed fear.
He is the four directions and his nature is profound.
He extends in all four directions and in between as well. [100]

He is without beginning and is the earth and the sky.
He is the lord of Lakshmi.
He is handsome, and his bracelets shine brightly.
He is the father and the first-born.
He is awesome, of terrifying valor. [101]

He is the resting place of all supports,
Yet he himself needs no support.
His smile is like a budding flower.
He is the watchman who never sleeps.
He moves upwards and walks the good path.
He gives life and is the cosmic sound.
He is the wager made in a game of chance. [102]

He is the standard and the reservoir of vitality.
He supports the breath of life and is the life-giving force.
He is the reality of each thing,
And knows the true nature of each thing.
His Self is one.
He is beyond birth, death, and old age. [103]

He is the earth, the sky, and the heavens.
He is the savior, the impeller, and the grandfather.
He is sacrifice and the lord of the sacrifice.

He is the one who offers and the means of the offering.
The sacrifice is his vehicle. [104]

All acts of sacrifice are his,
For he supports and fashions the sacrifice.
He accepts the sacrifice and is the reason it is offered;
He ends the sacrifice and is its mystery.
He is food and verily the enjoyer of food. [105]

He is self-created, born of his own Self.
When born as the boar he dug up the earth.
He may be heard in the chanting of the Veda.
He brings joy to his mother Devaki.
He is the creator, the lord of the earth;
He destroys evil. [106]

He carries a conch and the sword Nandaki,
And also the discus and the bow of horn.
He carries a mace and is a fearless charioteer.
He never wavers, and fights with all good weapons. [107]

We worship the Infinite, whose forms are countless.
We meditate upon the eternal Spirit,
Who has a thousand feet, a thousand eyes,
A thousand heads, a thousand names.
We bow in prayer before the one who has
Sustained the worlds through the countless eons of time.

Earnestly, with my whole heart,
I offer to that Supreme Being whatsoever I do:
All my actions, words, and thoughts,
The work of my senses and my intellect,
And my very soul.

An Eight-Step Program

The following paragraphs present the eight-step program for spiritual living which I have found effective in my own life. These steps are elaborated much more fully in my book *Meditation,* which has a full chapter on each step, and in a set of four audio cassettes entitled *The Theory and Practice of Meditation.*

I. MEDITATION

The heart of this program is meditation: half an hour every morning, as early as is convenient. Do not increase this period; if you want to meditate more, have half an hour in the evening also, preferably at the very end of the day.

Set aside a room in your home to be used only for meditation and spiritual reading. After a while that room will become associated with meditation in your mind, so that simply entering it will have a calming effect. If you cannot spare a room, have a particular corner. Whichever you choose, keep your meditation place clean, well ventilated, and reasonably austere.

Sit in a straight-backed chair or on the floor and gently close your eyes. If you sit on the floor, you may need to support your back lightly against a wall. You should be comfortable enough to forget your body, but not so comfortable that you become drowsy.

Whatever position you choose, be sure to keep your

head, neck, and spinal column erect in a straight line. As concentration deepens, the nervous system relaxes and you may begin to fall asleep. It is important to resist this tendency right from the beginning, by drawing yourself up and away from your back support until the wave of sleep has passed.

Once you have closed your eyes, begin to go *slowly,* in your mind, through one of the passages from the scriptures or the great mystics which I recommend for use in meditation. I usually suggest learning first the Prayer of Saint Francis of Assisi:

> Lord, make me an instrument of thy peace.
> Where there is hatred, let me sow love;
> Where there is injury, pardon;
> Where there is doubt, faith;
> Where there is despair, hope;
> Where there is darkness, light;
> Where there is sadness, joy.
>
> O Divine Master, grant that I may not so much seek
> To be consoled as to console,
> To be understood as to understand,
> To be loved as to love;
> For it is in giving that we receive,
> It is in pardoning that we are pardoned,
> It is in dying [to self] that we are born to eternal life.

Do not follow any association of ideas or try to think about the passage. If you are giving your attention to each word, the meaning cannot help sinking in. When distractions come, do not resist them, but give more attention to the words of the passage. If your mind strays from the passage entirely, bring it back gently to the beginning and start again.

When you reach the end of the passage, you may use it again as necessary to complete your period of meditation until you have memorized others. It is helpful to have a wide variety of passages for meditation, drawn from the world's major traditions. Each passage should be positive and practical, drawn from a major scripture or from a mystic of the highest stature. I especially recommend:

* the Twenty-third Psalm
* the Shema
* the Lord's Prayer
* the Beatitudes
* Saint Paul's "Epistle on Love" (1 Corinthians 13)
* Thomas a Kempis, *Imitation of Christ* III. 5
  ("The Wonderful Effects of Divine Love")
* from the Dhammapada of the Buddha, the first and
  last chapters
* from the Bhagavad Gita:
    2.54–72 ("The Illumined Man")
    9.26–34 ("Make It an Offering")
    12.1–20 ("The Way of Love")
    18.49–73 ("Be Aware of Me Always")
* Ansari of Herat, "Invocations"
* Jalaluddin Rumi, "I Am the Dust in the Sunlight"

These and many other beautiful passages from the world's religions can be found in my collection *God Makes the Rivers to Flow*.

The secret of meditation is simple: we become what we meditate on. When you use the Prayer of Saint Francis every day in meditation, you are driving the words deep into your consciousness. Eventually they become an integral part of your personality, which means they will find constant expression in what you do, what you say, and what you think.

For those who like to get their instructions in person, I have taken a cue from technology and offered the next best thing. My videotape *Meditation* gives these basic instructions with many practical illustrations and suggestions. A second videotape, *On the Seabed of the Unconscious,* gives a look at what happens when meditation has taken you to the very depths of the mind.

2. REPETITION OF THE MANTRAM

A mantram, or Holy Name, is a powerful spiritual formula which has the capacity to transform consciousness when it is repeated silently in the mind. There is nothing magical about this. It is simply a matter of practice, as you can verify for yourself.

Every religious tradition has a mantram, often more

than one. For Christians the name of Jesus itself is a powerful mantram. Catholics also use *Hail Mary* or *Ave Maria*. Jews may use *Barukh attah Adonai,* "Blessed art thou, O Lord," or the Hasidic formula *Ribono shel olam,* "Lord of the universe." Muslims repeat the name of Allah or *Allahu akbar,* "God is great." Probably the oldest Buddhist mantram is *Om mani padme hum,* referring to the "jewel in the lotus of the heart." In Hinduism, among many choices, I recommend *Rama, Rama, Rama,* which was Mahatma Gandhi's mantram, or the longer mantram I received from my own spiritual teacher, my grandmother:

> *Haré Rama, Haré Rama,*
> *Rama Rama, Haré Haré,*
> *Haré Krishna, Haré Krishna,*
> *Krishna Krishna, Haré Haré.*

Select a mantram that appeals to you deeply. In many traditions, it is customary to take the mantram used by your spiritual teacher. Then, once you have chosen, do not change your mantram. Otherwise you will be like a person digging shallow holes in many places; you will never go deep enough to find water.

Repeat your mantram silently whenever you get the chance: while walking, while waiting, while doing mechanical chores like washing dishes, and especially when you are falling asleep. You will find that this is not mindless repetition; the mantram will help to keep you relaxed and alert.

Whenever you are angry or afraid, nervous or worried or resentful, repeat the mantram until the agitation subsides. The mantram works to steady the mind, and all these emotions are power running against you which the mantram can harness and put to work.

3. SLOWING DOWN

Hurry makes for tension, insecurity, inefficiency, and superficial living. To guard against hurrying through the day, start the day early and simplify your life so that you do not try to fill your time with more than you can do.

When you find yourself beginning to speed up, repeat your mantram to help you slow down.

It is important here not to confuse slowness with sloth, which breeds carelessness, procrastination, and general inefficiency. In slowing down we should attend meticulously to details, giving our very best even to the smallest undertaking.

4. ONE-POINTEDNESS

Doing more than one thing at a time divides attention and fragments consciousness. When we read and eat at the same time, for example, part of our mind is on what we are reading and part on what we are eating; we are not getting the most from either activity. Similarly, when talking with someone, give him or her your full attention. These are little things, but all together they help to unify consciousness and deepen concentration.

Everything we do should be worthy of our full attention. When the mind is one-pointed it will be secure, free from tension, and capable of the concentration that is the mark of genius in any field.

5. TRAINING THE SENSES

In the food we eat, the books and magazines we read, the movies we see, all of us are subject to the dictatorship of rigid likes and dislikes. To free ourselves from this conditioning, we need to learn to change our likes and dislikes freely when it is in the best interests of those around us or ourselves. We should choose what we eat by what our body needs, for example, rather than by what the taste buds demand. Similarly, the mind eats too, through the senses. In this age of mass media, we need to be very discriminating in what we read and what we go to see for entertainment; for we become in part what our senses take in.

6. PUTTING OTHERS FIRST

Dwelling on ourselves builds a wall between ourselves and others. Those who keep thinking about *their* needs, *their* wants, *their* plans, *their* ideas cannot help becoming lonely and insecure. The simple but effective technique I recommend is to learn to put other people first—beginning within the circle of your family and friends, where there is already a basis of love on which to build. When husband and wife try to put each other first, for example, they are not only moving closer to each other. They are also removing the barriers of their ego-prison, which deepens their relationships with everyone else as well.

7. READING IN WORLD MYSTICISM

We are so surrounded today by a low concept of what the human being is that it is essential to give ourselves a higher image. For this reason I recommend half an hour or so each day to reading the scriptures and the writings of the great mystics of all religions. Just before bedtime, after evening meditation, is a particularly good time, because the thoughts you fall asleep in will be with you throughout the night.

There is a helpful distinction between works of inspiration and works of spiritual instruction. Inspiration may be drawn from every tradition or religion. Instructions in meditation and other spiritual disciplines, however, can differ from and even seem to contradict each other. For this reason, it is wise to confine instructional reading to the works of one teacher or path. Choose your teacher carefully. A good teacher lives what he or she teaches, and it is the student's responsbility to exercise sound judgment. Then, once you have chosen, give your teacher your full loyalty.

8. SPIRITUAL ASSOCIATION

The Sanskrit word for this is *satsang*, "association with those who are spiritually oriented." When we are trying to change our life, we need the support of others with the same goal. If you have friends who are meditating along the lines suggested here, it is a big help to meditate together regularly. Many people associated with me meet like this every week or two. Before meditation, they often listen to a tape of one of my talks.

Share your times of entertainment too. Relaxation is an important part of spiritual living.

By practicing this eightfold program sincerely and systematically, as I can testify from my own personal experience, it is possible for everyone to realize the supreme goal of life. Even a little such practice, the Gita says, begins to transform personality, leading to profoundly beneficial changes in ourselves and in the world around us.

Glossary & Guide
to Sanskrit Pronunciation

Consonants. Consonants are generally pronounced as in English, but there are some differences. Sanskrit has many so-called aspirated consonants, that is, consonants pronounced with a slight *h* sound. For example, the consonant *ph* is pronounced as English *p* followed by an *h* as in ha*ph*azard; *bh* is as in a*bh*or. The aspirated consonants are *kh, gh, ch, jh, th, dh, ph, bh.*

h	as in	*h*ome
g	" "	*g*old
j	" "	*J*une

The other consonants are approximately as in English.

Vowels. Every Sanskrit vowel has two forms, one short and one long. The long form is pronounced twice as long as the short. In the English transliteration the long vowels are marked with a bar (¯). The diphthongs—*e, ai, o, au*—are also pronounced twice as long as the short vowels. Thus, in the words *nīla* "blue" and *gopa* "cowherd," the first syllable is held twice as long as the second.

a	as in	*u*p	*ri*	as in	w*ri*tten
ā	" "	f*a*ther	*e*	" "	th*ey*
i	" "	g*i*ve	*ai*	" "	*ai*sle
ī	" "	s*ee*	*o*	" "	g*o*
u	" "	p*u*t	*au*	" "	c*ow*
ū	" "	r*u*le			

THE SPELLING OF SANSKRIT WORDS

To simplify the spelling of Sanskrit words we have used a minimum of diacritical marks, retaining only the long mark (¯) for the long vowels and omitting the other diacritics which are some-

times used in rendering Sanskrit words into English. Some sub-
tleties of Sanskrit pronunciation, such as the difference between
retroflex and dental consonants, are therefore lost. The gain in
simplicity, however, seems to outweigh this loss.

Glossary

ajapa-japam   The MANTRAM or Holy Name repeating itself in the consciousness of the devotee, without personal effort.

Arjuna   A hero of the MAHABHARATA, where he is the beloved disciple and friend of KRISHNA. The BHAGAVAD GITA is Sri Krishna's personal instruction to Arjuna.

avatāra   The descent of God to earth; the incarnation of God on earth, as RAMA and KRISHNA are regarded as *avatar*s or incarnations of VISHNU.

Bhagavad Gītā ["The Song of the Lord"]   One of the most widely revered of the Hindu scriptures, in which Sri KRISHNA, representing the Lord within, gives spiritual instruction to ARJUNA, a warrior prince who stands for every aspiring human being.

Bhāgavatam   An ancient and popular work in Sanskrit verse which narrates the legends of VISHNU's incarnations, including his appearance as KRISHNA.

Brahman   The attributeless Godhead, the supreme reality underlying existence.

Buddha   "One who is awake"; the title given to Siddhartha Gautama (ca. 563–480 B.C.) after he attained NIRVANA, Self-realization.

dharma   The universal law which holds all life together in unity; duty, the highest obligations of one's nature and position.

Eckhart, Johannes (1260–1327)   (Usually "Meister" or "Master" Eckhart) A Dominican mystic and theologian of Germany, one of the loftiest figures in world mysticism.

Francis de Sales, Saint (1567–1622)   A Carmelite priest and mystic who taught that God could be found by ordinary people leading busy lives in the world of business and family.

Francis of Assisi, Saint (1182–1226) Perhaps the most universally loved of Christian saints. His simplicity, love, and selfless service inspired the creation of three great Franciscan orders in his own time, and continue to inspire aspirants of all backgrounds today.

Gandhi, Mohandas K. (1869–1948) (Usually "Mahatma Gandhi"; the title *Mahatma* means "great soul.") Revered as the man who led India to freedom through nonviolence and selfless service, Gandhi is also one of the world's most original and practical mystics, whose contributions to politics and economics are acutely relevant today.

Ganesha The Lord as remover of obstacles, whose elephant head symbolizes immense power. Most Hindu temples have a shrine to him. In mythology he is the child of Shiva and Parvati.

Gita BHAGAVAD GITA

guru A spiritual teacher.

japam Repetition of the MANTRAM or Holy Name.

John of the Cross, Saint (1542–1591) A Spanish Carmelite mystic, one of the great figures in world mysticism. He was confessor, disciple, and friend to Saint TERESA OF AVILA. His spiritual journey is reflected in his books and poems, notably *The Ascent of Mount Carmel, The Dark Night of the Soul,* and *Spiritual Canticle.*

Julian of Norwich (b. 1343, d. after 1413) An English mystic and Benedictine anchoress whose spiritual experiences, recorded in *Revelations of Divine Love,* are a classic of spiritual literature.

Kabir (c. 1440–1518) Mystic and poet of India, claimed and revered by both Hindus and Muslims.

karma (Literally "something done") Action; the results of action; the sum of the consequences of what one has done, said, and thought. The "law of karma" holds that consequences are implicit in every action, as a tree is in a seed, and have to unfold when circumstances are right: "As ye sow, so shall ye reap."

Krishna An incarnation of VISHNU, who chose to be born on earth to alleviate suffering and re-establish DHARMA, righteousness. In his divine aspect, Krishna is the Lord himself; in his human aspect, he is a young man in Indian antiquity who grew up in seclusion as a cowherd boy, then slew the despotic king Kamsa and assumed his kingdom. In the MAHABHARATA (particularly the BHAGAVAD GITA) he is Arjuna's friend and teacher.

Lankavatāra Sutra A Mahayana Buddhist scripture, of special importance in Zen.

Mahābhārata   An epic poem relating the story of the struggle of YUDHISHTHIRA, ARJUNA, and their brothers to gain their usurped kingdom. This vast poem is a treasury of Hindu myth, legend, and spiritual wisdom. Among many other classics, it includes the *Thousand Names of Vishnu* and the BHAGAVAD GITA.

mantram   A Holy Name or sacred phrase; a spiritual formula repeated to concentrate the mind. (*See* "An Eight-Step Program," page 313.)

māyā   The illusion of separateness; appearance, the phenomenal world, as opposed to the changeless reality called BRAHMAN.

meditation   The practice of training the mind to dwell on a single interior focus at will, until the mind becomes completely absorbed in the object of contemplation and is stilled.

Mīrā (1547–1614)   One of India's best-loved mystics and poets, famed for her songs of love and longing for KRISHNA. She was a princess of Chitore but renounced everything to live a life of devotion in VRINDAVAN.

moksha   Liberation, release from all spiritual and mental fetters; the goal of the spiritual life.

nirvāna   Extinction of self-will, Self-realization, MOKSHA.

Om (or aum)   A sacred syllable, the Holy Word signifying BRAHMAN, the impersonal Godhead, in the Hindu scriptures. Often uttered at the beginning and end of invocations and as part of a MANTRAM or Holy Name.

Patanjali (2nd cent. B.C.?)   Author of the *Yoga Sutras,* the most important ancient work on *raja yoga,* the path of meditation. One of the best translations is *How to Know God,* translated by Swami Prabhavananda and Christopher Isherwood.

prāna   Breath; vitality, life, vital energy; the undifferentiated energy of which all forms of energy in the universe are expressions.

purusha   "Person"; the Self, the soul, the deathless core of personality.

Rāma   In his divine aspect, the Lord himself, one of the most widely loved forms of God in India; historically, a prince in ancient India whose story is told in the RAMAYANA. He is worshipped as an incarnation of VISHNU, who came to earth to destroy the evil king Ravana.

Rāmakrishna (1836–1886)   A Bengali saint loved all over India, whose universal vision inspired a renaissance of mysticism in India and around the world. Ramakrishna taught, and lived out in his own life, that God can be realized within any of the world's great religions if one seeks with completely unified desire. His teachings to householders can be found in *The Gospel of Sri Ramakrishna,* by "M," a direct disciple.

Rāmana Mahārshi (1879–1950) A famous sage of South India, whose lofty stature and nondogmatic method of self-inquiry attracted many Western seekers.

Rāmāyana An ancient epic popular throughout India, which tells the story of RAMA, an incarnation of Vishnu, and his quest for Sita, his beloved wife, who was abducted by the demon king Ravana. Their story and character embody the ideals of Hindu society.

Rāmdās (1884–1963) A contemporary saint who traveled throughout India practicing and teaching Self-realization through repetition of the Holy Name. His pilgrimages are described in *In Search of God, In the Vision of God,* and *World is God.*

Rig Veda The earliest of the VEDAS, the ancient scriptures of India. The oldest of its hymns date back to the second millennium B.C., if not earlier.

sādhana A body of disciplines which leads to Self-realization.

samadhi The unitive state, Self-realization; the climax of meditation, in which the barriers between oneself and the Lord disappear.

samskāra A deep mental impression produced by past experiences, a compulsive pattern of thought and behavior.

Shankara A name of Shiva; also a great mystic and philosopher from South India, who inspired a revival of faith in the Hindu scriptures sometime between the sixth and eighth century A.D.

soma A drink used in ancient Indian rituals; the drink of the gods; also, personified, the deity of that ritual and its effects.

Srī [pronounced "shri"] Beauty, auspiciousness, etc.; a title of respect; personified, the goddess of beauty and good fortune, VISHNU'S consort.

Teresa of Avila, Saint (1515–1582) One of the best loved of Catholic saints, a great mystic who combined insight with practicality and a human touch. With Saint JOHN OF THE CROSS, she inspired a renaissance of spirituality in the Carmelite movement that continues today.

Traherne, Thomas (c. 1634–1674) English mystic poet, best remembered for his *Centuries of Meditations.*

Upanishads Mystical writings, part of the VEDAS, which record the spiritual discoveries of the sages of ancient India.

Vedas   The scriptures of the Hindus, regarded by the orthodox as direct revelation. The oldest is the RIG VEDA.

Vishnu   God as Preserver, second in the Hindu Trinity, who
incarnates himself in every age for the establishment of
righteousness or DHARMA. His most widely worshipped
incarnations are RAMA and KRISHNA. (See also Introduc-
tion)

Vrindāvan   The village where KRISHNA spent his childhood
as a cowherd, revered for centuries as a place of pil-
grimage.

Yoga Sutras   See under PATANJALI.

Yudhishthira   Eldest brother of ARJUNA in the MAHA-
BHARATA, respected by all as the soul of righteousness or
DHARMA.